A Naknek Chronicle

Ten Thousand Years in a Land of Lakes and Rivers and Mountains of Fire

Looking up Iliuk Arm toward the mouth of the Savonoski River, Mt. Katolinat on the right. View from Mt. Dumpling.

Don E. Dumond

Upper Knife Creek in flood stage, photo by Victor Cahalane, 1954.

CONTENTS

                                                                        Page

List of Illustrations iv

List of Tables v

Foreword vi

Preface ix

1. THE PLACE 1

    Shape of the Land 1

    Toward Archaeology 6

    Notes to Chapter 1 11

2. THE MORE ANCIENT PAST 13

    The Earliest People in Alaska 13

    Hunters on the Alaska Peninsula: The Paleoarctic Tradition 15

    Later Hunters: The Northern Archaic Tradition 17

    Earliest Known People at Brooks River: The Kittiwick Period 20

        Brooks River Strand Phase 21

        Brooks River Beachridge Phase 23

    First Heavy Use of Brooks River: The Gomer Period 24

    Increasing Use of the Upper Drainage: The Brooks River Period 29

        Smelt Creek Phase 30

        Brooks River Weir Phase 32

        Brooks River Falls Phase 33

        Discussion: The Brooks River Period 34

    Expansion in the Lower Drainage: The Naknek Period 35

        Brooks River Camp Phase 36

        Brooks River Bluffs Phase 41

        Pavik Phase: The Advent of the Russians 46

        Unexplored Sites of the Upper Drainage 51

    Notes to Chapter 2 55

3. THE NINETEENTH CENTURY 59

    Maps 59

    Ethnic Groups 60

    Settlements and Population 63

    Households and Families 69

    Visitors 71

        Ivan Petroff 71

        The Earl of Lonsdale 74

        The Frank Leslie Alaska Expedition 75

        Josiah Edward Spurr 76

        Other Travelers 77

    Notes to Chapter 3 79

Page

4. WHEN THE CENTURY TURNED 83

    Fish Business 83

    The Latest Great Eruption 84

    Families 88

        Severnovsk Settlements 88

        Naknek River Villages 91

    Influenza 93

    Notes to Chapter 4 96

5. INTO THE TWENTIETH 99

    Notes to Chapter 5 101

    REFERENCES 102

Afterword 109

ILLUSTRATIONS

Figures   Page

1. The northern Alaska Peninsula 1

2. The fronts of Pleistocene-age glaciers and glacial Lake Naknek 2

3. Brooks River and the Aleutian Range 4

4. Katmai Project archaeologists testing at Kukak village site 5

5. Stratigraphy at the Kukak village site, 1965 7

6. Volcanic ash and cultural phases 8

7. The lower Naknek drainage system 9

8. Excavations at the "crystal palace," Brooks River 10

9. James VanStone at Paugvik 12

10. The North Pacific region 13

11. Microblades and wedge-shaped cores of the Paleoarctic tradition 14

12. Ugashik Narrows 16

13. Core and blades of the Aleutian Islands 17

14. Use of the dart throwing board or atlatl 18

15. Paleoarctic and Northern Archaic camps at Kukaklek Lake 19

16. Stone projectile points of the Northern Archaic tradition 19

17. River and lake terraces around Brooks River 20

18. Test pits in the woods 21

19. Tent floor of the Brooks River Strand phase 22

20. Artifacts of the Brooks River Strand phase 23

21. Plan and cross-sections of a house of the Brooks River Gravels phase 25

22. Artifacts of the Brooks River Gravels phase 26

23. Excavating at the Smelt Creek site 29

24. Stone artifacts of the Brooks River period 31

25. Reconstructed pots of the Brooks River period 32

26. Plan and sections of a house of the Brooks River Weir phase 33

27. Stone vessel of the Brooks River Weir phase 34

28. Shapes of pottery from Brooks River 36

29. Stone artifacts of the Brooks River Camp phase 37

30. Plan and sections of a house of the Brooks River Camp phase 38

31. Bone and antler artifacts of the Brooks River Camp phase 39

32. Stone artifacts of the Brooks River Bluffs phase 42

33. Designs engraved on pebbles, Brooks River Bluffs phase 43

34. Plan of a pair of houses of the Brooks River Bluffs phase 45

35. Plan of the Paugvik site 48

36. Excavating at the Paugvik site 50

37. Artifacts of the Pavik phase 51

38. Sod-covered houses at the Severnovsk village of Nunamiut, 1918 53

39. People of the lower Naknek River, 1827-1828 58

40. Composite map of Vasil'ev, 1829-1831 59

41. Distribution of nineteenth-century Native ethnic groups 61

42. The chapel at abandoned Nunamiut, 1919 65

43. Native village west of the Naknek Packing Co., 1900 66

44. View of Iliuk Arm according to Ivan Petroff 73

45. The Lonsdale party moving toward Katmai Pass, 1889 74

46. Map of the crossing of Katmai Pass, 1898 77

47. The plant of the Naknek Packing Co., 1900 83

48. Tents of Native people along the Naknek River, 1919 84

49. Area of heavy volcanic ash fall, June 1912 85

50. The chapel at abandoned Nunamiut, 1940 86

51. The slumped roof of a house at abandoned Nunamiut, 1953 87

52. Native village west of the Arctic Packing Co. (APA), 1900 91

53. The Arctic Packing Co. (APA), 1900 94

54. Pelagia Melgenak, Savonoski, 1961 98

55. Billy Hill family at Libbyville cannery, 1940 109

TABLES

1. Native Births by Ethnic Group, to 1897 62

2. Enumerated Native Population of the Naknek Drainage, 1850 - 1910 63

FOREWORD

Archaeologists, generally speaking, are an interesting hybrid of scientist, adventurer, detective and educator. We are fascinated by ancient cultures far beyond the reach of memory and recorded history. We are trained in the ways of discovering and recovering the limited material remains at archaeological sites and then deciphering meaning from the evidence to understand what really happened and why. No matter how careful we are in examining and manipulating the data, more often than not we can only guess at how to translate what we find into terms of human behavior and cultural meaning. Through our cautious and hard-won insights, most archaeologists develop a profound respect for the ingenuity and expertise of prehistoric peoples.

Archaeologists are conservationists, too, because we know that we have much to learn from the past. The archaeological record is fragile and already damaged by the passage of time and by history, from both natural and cultural agents. Keep in mind that this 10,000-year-long story of human occupation in the Naknek River area is told from less than 200 known sites in the region, only a small fraction of which have been excavated or even tested. One must consider the large amount of time and the random snapshot of past behavior that each site represents, to appreciate how valuable every archaeological site is. The link between the prehistoric past and present Native people through oral tradition has been broken and this is another reason why the science of archaeology and the protection of archaeological sites are so important. Just as essential is sharing this knowledge with the public, in whose trust these archaeological resources reside.

It is within the context of these principles that Don E. Dumond., Professor Emeritus of Anthropology at the University of Oregon, undertook the task of relating the prehistory of the Naknek River region for the public on behalf of the National Park Service and encouraged by long-time local education leader, Frank Hill. The Naknek River drainage, a rich mosaic of lakes, streams, wetlands and mountains, forms the heart of the four-million acre Katmai National Park and Preserve. Archaeological research in this region spans the last fifty years and while it is well represented in the professional literature, there are few resources for local residents, students, teachers and visitors to draw upon.

Professor Dumond began research in the region 45 years ago and has worked along the Naknek River from the Savonoski River and Brooks Camp to Paugvik at the river mouth. He has remained an active and valued participant in and advisor to Katmai's cultural resources program. *A Naknek Chronicle* provides firsthand accounts of surprising archaeological discoveries and tells a fascinating story, punctuated by volcanic eruptions and floods, pixies and small tools, strange newcomers and unexplained disappearances, and puzzling engravings on river pebbles.

The author draws from his extensive research and knowledge of prehistory across Alaska and Siberia to understand the region's prehistory in the context of the larger world. Hooked by his dedication to public education and service to archaeology, he agreed to cover not only the archaeology and prehistory with which he is so familiar, but to extend his narrative into the early twentieth century, ending with occurrences such as the volcanic eruption in the vicinity of Mt. Katmai, the outbreak of influenza in 1919, and the signs of early growth of the fishing industry. After that time, the great influx of outsiders to the region tangles the threads of history considerably. Information about the late nineteenth century villages now within Katmai is derived largely from intensive research in progress for the National Park Service by Katherine L. Arndt of the University of Alaska, Fairbanks.

This history, covering the period from about 8000 BC to the 1920s, is presented in these pages. Following it in the Afterword is the report of a biographic interview with Frank Hill, former Superintendent of the Lake and Peninsula School District and currently the Vice President for Education with the Alaska Federation of Natives. In a very general way Mr. Hill's story can be taken as representative of that of the many people whose family members first appeared in the Naknek region after 1920, and who now are seen as old timers. It is hoped that this book will serve as a primary resource for teachers of Alaska History and that it will inspire student interest in the prehistory and history of this great region.

Jeanne M. Schaaf
Chief, Cultural Resources
Lake Clark and Katmai National Parks and Preserves

Author on left with NPS Ranger-Pilot Tom O'Hara, photo by Dale Vinson summer 2001. As an Alaska Native and life-long resident of the Alaska Peninsula Tom brought his cultural heritage and his very considerable geographical knowledge to National Park Service management policy. It is the hope of the National Park Service that Tom's life will inspire upcoming generations of young Alaskans to a life of public service helping to manage public lands in Alaska.

Preface

My involvement with the archaeology of the Naknek region began in 1960 — not a little to my surprise as a graduate student at the University of Oregon — when the archaeology of Brooks River was suddenly offered to me as a Ph.D. dissertation topic, with expenses provided by a National Science Foundation grant to my academic adviser plus additional assistance from what was then the Bureau of Commercial Fisheries of the U.S. Fish and Wildlife Service. From that date through the present year I have been regularly, if at times intermittently, involved with the Naknek River region in the study of its early archaeology, and also an effort to understand its history over the most recent couple of centuries. The course of this work, especially the earth-moving part, is a little more fully described in the first chapter of the pages that follow, before I go on to summarize the major things that I have learned about the area over these forty-five years.

In that time debts have accumulated to many people whom I have tried to acknowledge here in text and notes. Not so listed, but who should be mentioned, are Dr. George Y. Harry, the 1960s director of the Bureau of Commercial Fisheries (later National Marine Fisheries) laboratory at Auke Bay, and Dr. L. S. Cressman, my mentor at the University of Oregon, who were together responsible for the run of luck that began with my arrival at Brooks River in 1960. Also not so listed, because there were simply too many of them, are members of the crews I fielded between 1960 and 1998, most of them students at the University of Oregon. I acknowledge their crucial help, even though it must here be anonymous.

Financial supporters, which have included the National Park Service at times, have been acknowledged scrupulously in the series of reports issued on the work in the Naknek River drainage area, nearly all of which are listed in the present references; they need not be detailed again. I must, however, signal out a few individuals to whom I owe specific debts of gratitude.

Insofar as archaeology is concerned, I have been somewhat peripherally involved with three National Park Service projects at Brooks River, all of which are drawn on for some of the present details. That of the early 1980s was directed by the late Harvey M. Shields, a National Park Service archaeologist and one-time student of mine, the report for which was prepared (and frequently acknowledged in references to follow) by a later student from the University of Oregon, Roger K. Harritt. In 1994, I worked with Patricia McClenahan, Katmai's first park archaeologist, and Richard Bland -- both former University of Oregon students – as we excavated portions of two houses on Brooks Lake. The project of 2001-2004 was directed by Katmai archaeologist Dale M. Vinson (who had been a crew member in the 1980s project under Shields), who was assisted by Barbara E. Bundy, another University of Oregon student, who was responsible for preparing the report

The outlet of Brooks River into Naknek Lake. Brooks Camp is on the north side of the river in the upper center of the photo. Photo taken in 1972 by Keith Trexler of the Alaska Task Force.

that is cited herein. I admit that I could not be even peripherally associated with projects such as these without horning in fairly decisively at times, and I thank them all for their forbearance.

Although I can take full responsibility for what I say about the archaeological background of the region, I am not so confident regarding matters of history. Whereas I have made constant efforts through the years to collect whatever information I could that pertains to the period after the arrival of Russian fur hunters in the region — a period beginning roughly with the opening of the nineteenth century — I am certainly deficient with regard to many details. I therefore must thank Dr. Kerry Feldman, of the University of Alaska Anchorage, who from two separate studies into matters of very recent history in the area has been most generous in allowing access to unpublished material. I am grateful also to Mary Jane Nielsen, whom I first met in South Naknek more than thirty years ago, and who then and later has been free to discuss her family and their heritage. Even more strongly, if possible, I must thank Dr. Katherine L. Arndt, now with the Archives section of the Alaska and Polar Regions Collections of the Elmer E. Rasmuson Library, the University of Alaska Fairbanks. Her knowledge of Russian documents relating to the place and period, which she has been so very generous in sharing, has been of more value than I can easily say in my completion of the present Chapter 3.

Finally, it is through a contract with the National Park Service that the writing of the present account has been completed. I thank them for the opportunity, and only hope the result at least partly matches their expectations. I especially aknowledge the efforts of Dr. Jeanne Schaaf, who served as my Park Service contact, who did some editing of the manuscript, added greatly to the number of illustrations, and served as go-between with the actual book designer. The appearance of the final product is due in very major ways to her inspiration.

Don E. Dumond

The Place

The Shape of the Land

The backbone of the Alaska Peninsula is the Aleutian Range, its volcanoes rising from a platform of much older, non-volcanic sedimentary rocks. Although it is the volcanoes rising into the skyline that give the mountain range its character, the low region to the northwest and west owes its form not to the volcanoes, but to the glaciers of the last major glacial period, the Pleistocene epoch. Within that lengthy span of ancient time there were repeated advances and retreats of the ice sheets that then capped the mountain ridge. It was the last major set of these advances — events commonly called the Late Glacial Maximum — that established today's character of lake systems and the tundra-covered lowlands that stretch from the lakes to the Bering Sea.

In the Naknek River region, this last ice maximum has been dated to the period between about 23,000 and 15,000 radiocarbon years ago, which would amount to about 24,000 and 14,000 BC according to the modern calendar.[1] At the height of this period the ice extended westward toward, but apparently did not reach, the present shore of Bristol Bay, leaving telltale glacial moraines and the lakes dammed behind them. On the east, however, it crossed what is now Shelikof Strait and covered essentially all of the Kodiak group of islands. So far as present information goes, it was somewhat after the end of this "maximum" period that humans made their first appearance in Alaska, and considerably later that they are known to have appeared on the Alaska Peninsula.

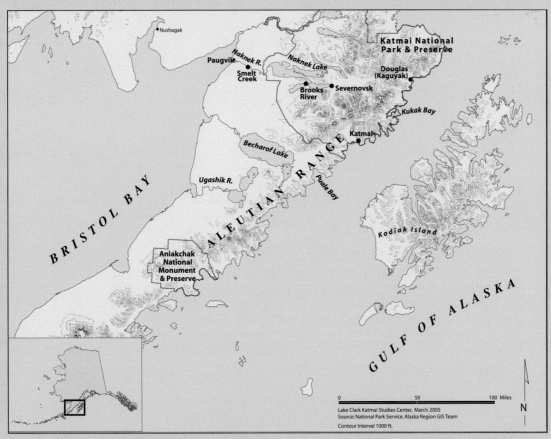

Figure 1 – *The Northern Alaska Peninsula. The Naknek drainage system is made up of Naknek River, Naknek Lake, and their tributaries. Places indicated by dots are abandoned villages or archaeological sites referred to in the text.*

1

THE PLACE – The Shape of the Land

Figure 2 diagrams aspects of the scarring of the Naknek River drainage region by ice, the details of which are drawn in large part from the first study of the extent of the glaciations, made more than 50 years ago, at which time the various ice advances then identified were named. By driving from the village of Naknek to Naknek Lake, one can recognize these moraine deposits as hills from which gravel has been mined, their age decreasing from west to east. Thus, what are designated the Johnston Hill and Mak Hill glaciations occurred earlier than the Late Glacial Maximum and its Brooks Lake glacial advance, which left the moraines

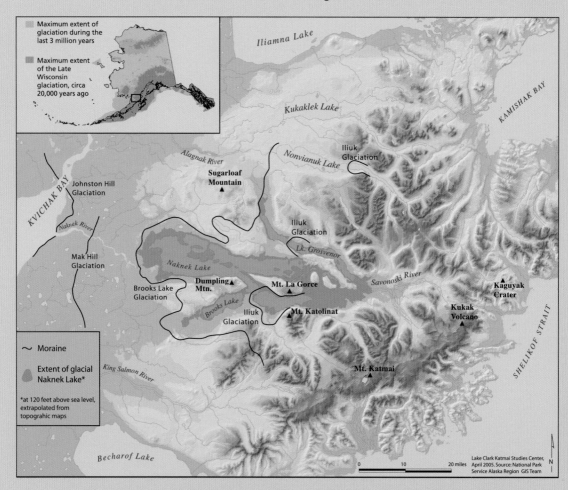

Figure 2 – Fronts of Pleistocene-age glaciers as shown by moraine deposits in the Naknek region and the approximate extent of glacial Lake Naknek The Brooks Lake glaciation scoured out the basins of most of the present lake systems of the Alaska Peninsula. Map inset shows the maximum extent of selected past glaciations

years ago   30,000   25,000

Beginning of the Last
Glacial Maximum

behind which the modern lakes of the Naknek system were formed. In the years since that first study, other researchers have suggested some revisions to the labels given as well at to the order of events. For instance, what are shown in Figure 2 as moraines of temporally separated Johnston Hill and Mak Hill advances are thought by certain investigators to have resulted from only a single complex set of events, and the Late Glacial Maximum has in turn been divided into four periods of ice advance or stades. Of these, the Brooks Lake glaciation has been declared a localized aspect of the second stade, termed the Iliamna advance; this deposited end-moraines that finally impounded the series of modern lakes that stretch from Iliamna Lake to the Ugashik lakes and beyond. Outwash of the Brooks Lake glaciation has been found to overlie tree parts that were dated by radiocarbon at about 26,000 years ago, and other researchers have suggested on the basis of various bits of evidence that all of these lake-forming glaciations were earlier than 16,000 years ago. This rather long period, 26,000 to 16,000 years ago, should therefore have witnessed the advance and, presumably, much of the retreat of the glaciation that formed the Naknek complex of lakes, although the much more limited Iliuk advance (Figure 2) may have been still somewhat later. [2]

In any event, the passing of the major glaciers recorded by geologists suggests that well before 10,000 BC the area was sufficiently ice-free to have been used by humans. This has been confirmed by radiocarbon ages derived from peat bored from near the bottoms of bogs that have formed in kettle lakes located on the tops of glacial deposits in the Naknek region.

One of these fossil bogs is near the very mouth of the Naknek River on Bristol Bay, another in the immediate vicinity of Kukak Bay on the Pacific, both of them yielding ice-free ages in excess of 9,000 radiocarbon years, or well before 8,000 BC. The age of nearly 8,000 radiocarbon years from a point on top of the moraine that impounds Naknek Lake itself was not from the base of the deep bog, but from compacted peat almost a foot above the gravel of that base, so that the figure follows the beginning of peat formation by an unknown number of years.

The earliest well-documented evidence of a human presence on the peninsula comes from research by University of Oregon archaeologists at the narrows between the Upper and Lower Ugashik lakes. So far there has been found only a hint of similar evidence in the vicinity of the Naknek system of lakes. The difference between the Naknek and the Ugashik lake systems in regard to preservation of such evidence is related to their elevations above sea level.

The modern elevation above sea level of both Ugashik lake surfaces is about 13 feet, or 4 meters. With tidal variation around Bristol Bay of 20 feet or so, the effects of high tides throughout most of the year are felt all the way up the Ugashik River to the

20,000   ▼   15,000

Land Bridge Open   End of the Last Glacial Maximum,
                          Brooks and Naknek Lake Moraines Formed by This Time

Figure 3 – Brooks River and the Aleutian Range looking east from Mt. Dumpling. The river, about a mile and a half in length, drains Brooks Lake (right) into Naknek Lake (left). Brooks Falls, a little more than five feet high, is approximately midway in the river's course. The far side of the river is now covered by spruce forest.

lakes themselves. The tides have therefore acted to control erosion, with the result that the modern narrows between the lakes, a well-known game crossing, is essentially unchanged from the time the lakes were first formed with the recession of the ice more than 10,000 years ago. The evidence of the earliest people, in short, is located in the same place as a concentration of evidence of many later peoples, including modern fishing and hunting camps. The first human presence recorded there was about 9,000 radiocarbon years ago, or around 8000 BC.[3]

Naknek Lake, on the other hand, has a surface elevation of some 34 feet (10 meters) above mean sea level, well above the extent of the highest high tide in Bristol Bay, the effects of which reach only to the rapids formed where the Naknek River flows over and through the moraine of the Brooks Lake glaciation. The great lake that was originally impounded behind that moraine was as much as 85 feet (26 meters) higher than the surface of Naknek Lake today, that single body of water covering what are modern Naknek, Brooks, Coville, and Grosvenor lakes. Well over 10,000 years ago the outlet of the lake into Naknek River began to erode downward, progressively lowering the level of the water and — as various ridges of rock were exposed — dividing what was left of the ancestral lake into the several modern bodies of water. Between Brooks and Naknek lakes, the area where the greater part of the archaeological research in the region has been concentrated, what is now Brooks River began as a narrows linking those two waters. At that time both of those two surfaces were roughly at the level of today's Brooks Lake, which has been mapped at near 60 feet (17 meters) above the sea — more than 21 feet above the modern Naknek Lake surface. At that time the narrows would have provided a restricted place for game to cross, and

years ago   15,000   10,000

| Land Bridge Open | First Evidence of People in Alaska | Alaska Peninsula is Largely Ice-Free | First Evidence of People on the Alaska Peninsula |

would almost certainly have been attractive to any early people who sought their living by hunting — just as attractive as the Ugashik Narrows.

But as Naknek Lake continued to lower, Brooks Lake was held up by the rocks at its outlet, and the present short river began to be formed, looping back and forth until the water had dropped to the rock ridge that creates Brooks Falls, by which time the course of the upper river, one can truthfully say, was set in stone. The river below the falls has continued its meandering and eroding course, following the steadily lowering level of Naknek Lake into the present. The result of all this movement is that extensive areas that were once on that original narrows or on the bank of the evolving river are now well away from the present channel and lake shores scattered over a complex set of terraces. Many are also now covered by forest (Figure 3), so that places where the most ancient inhabitants of the area would have chosen to camp is no longer even roughly clear from the conformation of the modern ground. As it stands, the earliest evidence of humans we have found along that river — Brooks River — is no more than about 4,400 radiocarbon years in the past, or a little earlier than 3000 BC. The campsites of that time, several of which we now know, are principally on former beach ridges on both sides of the river marking what was then the shore of Naknek Lake (about 20 feet, or a bit over 6 meters, above the modern level); they were, in other words, at what was then the river's mouth.

With this as an introduction to the region, we turn to early evidence of humans.

Figure 4 – Katmai Project archaeologists Wilbur "Buck" Davis (left) and J. W. Leach excavating a trench at the Kukak village site on the Katmai coast, 1953.

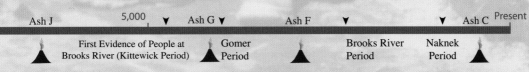

Ash J	5,000	Ash G ▼	Ash F ▼	Ash C	Present

First Evidence of People at Brooks River (Kittewick Period)   Gomer Period   Brooks River Period   Naknek Period

Toward Archaeology

If we pass over a brief visit to Naknek by a Smithsonian Institution anthropologist in the early 1930s, and a hole quickly dug in the old Paugvik village by a pair of archaeologists weathered into Naknek in 1948, serious archaeological research in the Naknek River region was begun in 1953, when the National Park Service sponsored its two-year Katmai Project. This also involved teams of geologists, volcanologists, and biologists marshaled to develop a preliminary inventory of the resources of what was then Katmai National Monument. The archaeologists were a two-man team from the University of Oregon who briefly examined and tested three settlements abandoned because of the volcanic eruption of 1912 — Katmai and Douglas villages on the Shelikof Strait coast and Severnovsk (often referred to in the American period as Savonoski) [4] on the upper Naknek River drainage system (Figure 4). In addition, they examined sites being revealed near the developing sport fishing camp at Brooks River; one of these they tested with a trench, and three others were located by surface indications. At the end of the season, they interviewed a former Severnovsk resident, Pelagia Melgenak, about her memories of the eruption of 1912.

Sustained archaeological research, however, waited several more years, until a separate project, partly sponsored by the Bureau of Commercial Fisheries of the U.S. Fish and Wildlife Service, allowed a second pair of archaeologists from the University of Oregon (myself and an assistant) to begin new research in 1960. The program would be continued by the University of Oregon, although somewhat intermittently, through the 1990s. Work at Brooks River and elsewhere in the region led to recognition of evidence not only of periods of human occupation from about 7000 BC to the late nineteenth century AD, but of an awe-inspiring series of volcanic deposits that were interspersed through time with campsites and houses of hunting and fishing people. Ten of these are designated volcanic ashes A (of 1912) through J (of sometime after 7,500 radiocarbon years ago, or about 6500 BC). The sequence of these events as reconstructed at Brooks River is diagrammed in Figure 6.

A word about terminology, as given in the figure: In order to allow archaeological collections to be sorted and then talked about, units of them are named with designations such as *phase*, or what some archaeologists refer to as *complex*. Usages vary somewhat, but most researchers use the term phase to refer to an assemblage of artifacts derived from a single place or limited region, representative of a relatively short span of time, and recognizably distinct from other groups of artifacts similarly defined. Ideally, the artifacts of a phase can be thought of as approximating the set of tools used by a single group of people at a single time. Although the area to which a phase pertains is restricted (as, for instance, the Naknek drainage area), the length of time it represents may vary considerably from place to place; in the Naknek region a phase inevitably covers several centuries, often five or even more. A tradition, on the other hand, is a unit of classification of apparently related collections (in terms of types of artifacts) that extend substantially through time, and it

Figure 5 – Don Dumond (left) and Harvey Rice study the stratigraphy exposed in excavations at the Kukak village site, 1965. The white ash from the 1912 eruption caps the black sediments in two house depressions. Photo by Paul Schumacher, National Park Service.

includes sequentially related phases and complexes found in various places over a broad geographic area — an area as great, say, as all of mainland Alaska, or even all of the arctic coasts of North America. Here, in addition, I refer to *periods* that include one or more separable phases and that relate only to the Naknek region. Thus, for instance, what is called the Brooks River period of the Naknek area is the time of three separate and sequential phases, all of them local manifestations of the Norton tradition (which appears all around the coast of mainland Alaska).

Although the phases and traditions will be taken up in the following chapter in order from early to late, the sites and collections of artifacts were certainly not recognized and excavated in that order — nor, for that matter, in reverse order, from late to early.

Rather, the trenches of 1953 at Severnovsk and Brooks River tapped, respectively, a late prehistoric site (Severnovsk) of what would be labeled the Brooks River Bluffs phase, and an earlier site (Brooks River) of what would become the Brooks River Camp phase.

When beginning work at Brooks River in 1960, we built on the Katmai Project results by turning to the eroding cutbank bluffs where house traces were exposed by the river. The resulting collections, appropriately enough, were designated the Brooks River Bluffs phase, later to be assigned to the local Naknek period and the Alaska-wide Thule tradition. But that same year we two archaeologists were housed in what was then the Fish and Wildlife Service building on the shores of Brooks Lake at the very head of Brooks

River. To take care of ourselves when it rained by having a noontime shelter and hot lunch, we also opened excavations in a promising depression on a former bank of the lake only fifty yards or so from the house. This revealed a semisubterranean habitation floor of what we named the Brooks River Weir phase (Brooks River period and Norton tradition) with reference to the FWS fish-counting weir then located at the head of Brooks River. Blind luck also struck when we found a trace at the gravel base of the Bluffs site of what we would know later as the Brooks River Gravels

phase of the Gomer period (and the Arctic Small Tool tradition).

Work the second season, 1961, was split between two parties. Three of us at Brooks River concentrated on a major site above Brooks Falls that we had identified the previous year, with rainy day excavations along the north shore of the river near the National Park Service headquarters, where we were staying. This led us to the naming of the Brooks River Falls phase, recovered from the first of these areas; to the recognition at the same site of two floors of the

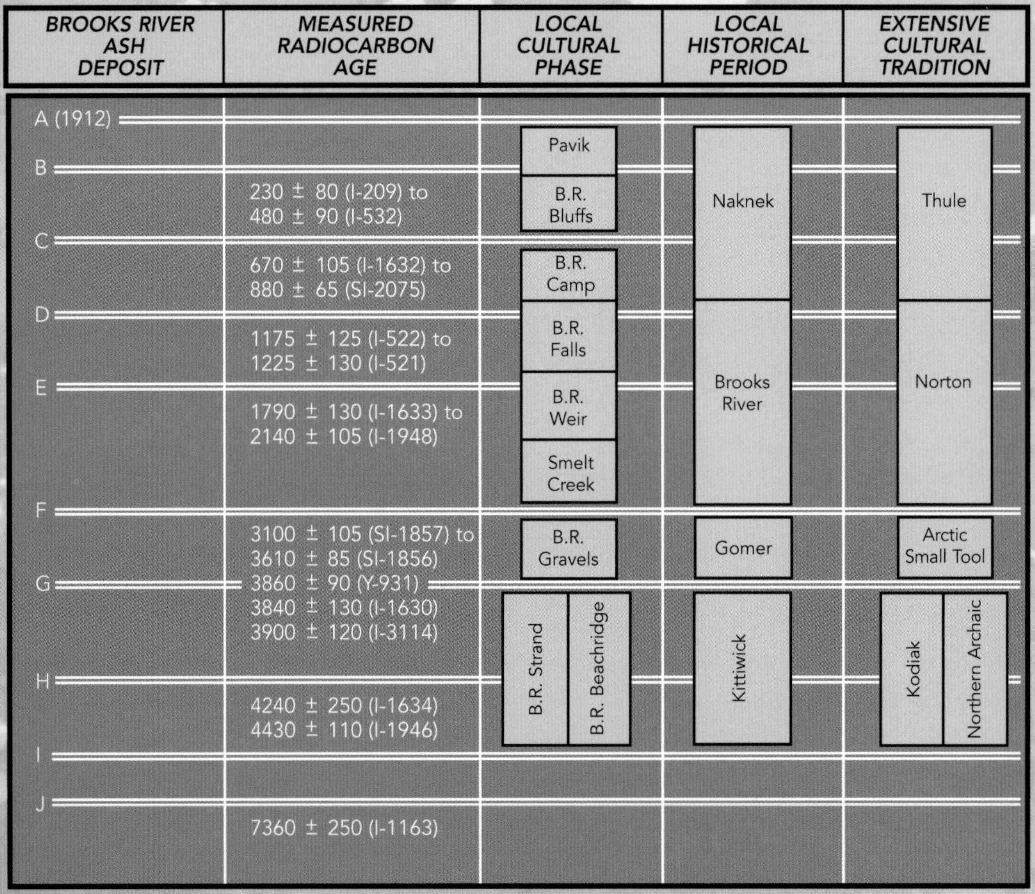

BROOKS RIVER ASH DEPOSIT	MEASURED RADIOCARBON AGE	LOCAL CULTURAL PHASE	LOCAL HISTORICAL PERIOD	EXTENSIVE CULTURAL TRADITION
A (1912)				
B		Pavik		
	230 ± 80 (I-209) to 480 ± 90 (I-532)	B.R. Bluffs	Naknek	Thule
C				
	670 ± 105 (I-1632) to 880 ± 65 (SI-2075)	B.R. Camp		
D				
	1175 ± 125 (I-522) to 1225 ± 130 (I-521)	B.R. Falls	Brooks River	Norton
E				
	1790 ± 130 (I-1633) to 2140 ± 105 (I-1948)	B.R. Weir		
		Smelt Creek		
F				
	3100 ± 105 (SI-1857) to 3610 ± 85 (SI-1856)	B.R. Gravels	Gomer	Arctic Small Tool
G	3860 ± 90 (Y-931) 3840 ± 130 (I-1630) 3900 ± 120 (I-3114)	B.R. Strand / B.R. Beachridge	Kittiwick	Kodiak / Northern Archaic
H				
	4240 ± 250 (I-1634) 4430 ± 110 (I-1946)			
I				
J				
	7360 ± 250 (I-1163)			

Figure 6 – Volcanic ash deposits, cultural phases, historical periods, and cultural traditions of the Naknek region of the past 8,000 years. The specific terms are explained in the text.

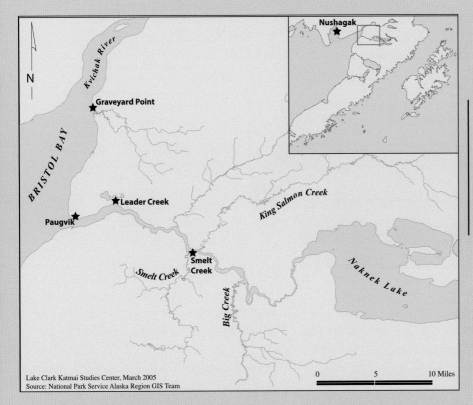

Figure 7 –
The lower
portion of the
Naknek drainage
system, showing
the locations
of some sites
mentioned.

Lake Clark Katmai Studies Center, March 2005
Source: National Park Service Alaska Region GIS Team

Gravels phase; and to the addition from our rainy day sites of two small components of the Weir phase. Meanwhile, a second team of three was led by Wilbur A. Davis, who had been a member of the 1953 team of archaeologists on the Katmai Project. This group worked from King Salmon along the lower Naknek River, locating and excavating a site near the mouth of Smelt Creek (from which was defined the Smelt Creek phase), and cutting a modest trench in the Paugvik village site (yielding material of the Pavik phase, named after the spelling that was published by the hit-and-run archaeologists of 1948).

The year 1963 then saw consolidation of our understanding of the archaeological sequence through efforts of a crew of seven at Brooks River, with work in deposits of all phases except Smelt Creek,

Brooks River Camp, and Pavik. In the previous summer, construction had begun on the road from Brooks River to the Valley of 10,000 Smokes. A spin-off came from the road borrow pits that had been bulldozed into every major river and lake terrace on the south side of Brooks River. It was the resulting exposures, together with extensive trenching at the Falls site in 1963, that led to understanding of the sequence of volcanic ashes shown in Figure 6.

By the end of that 1963 season, the sequence from the Gravels phase to the arrival of Europeans in the persons of Russian fur hunters was understood in its major outlines. At the same time, we were convinced that there was no earlier occupation to be found at Brooks River — nothing, that is, that would lie below the distinctive (yellow) volcanic ash G which is

Figure 8 – National Park Service excavations of a large Bluffs phase house called the "crystal palace" because of the discovery of a charred basket containing quartz crystals on the burned house floor, fall 1983. Left to right, Roger Harritt, Harvey Shields (excavation director), Fred Clark and Cindy Amdur. Photo by and courtesy of crew member Dale Vinson.

labeled in Figure 6. This notion was dispelled in 1964 and 1965 (as will be seen later) through encounters with both the Strand and Beachridge phases, and more especially in 1967 when the excavation of Camp phase houses led us to an extensive underlying and deeply buried camping area of the Brooks River Strand phase.

In the 1970s we spent two seasons on the Ugashik River to the southwest, where we found the earliest occupation thus far known on the Alaska Peninsula, dated at about 8000 BC. We also expanded work along the Naknek River and adjacent coast, where in addition to exploring sites related to those known at Brooks River we located a camping location with occupations dating to about 7000 and 5000 BC, designated the Koggiung and Graveyard phases, respectively. Parenthetically, the 1970s were also noteworthy for those of us on the Oregon crews: in that decade we were able to give up our tents in favor of real houses (in Naknek through the courtesy of the Chuck Hornbergers and the Leonard Mundorfs, at Ugashik through the generosity of Win Condict),

and for the first time the Oregon crews in Alaska included women as well as men, which added a bit to the tone of things.

In the 1980s the National Park Service turned to salvage excavations of a large Bluffs phase house threatened through continued erosion by Brooks River (Figure 8), while later in that decade we of the University of Oregon teamed with archaeologists of the Field Museum of Natural History of Chicago to conduct a season of excavation in the Paugvik village site near the mouth of the Naknek River (Figure 9). Although these projects changed nothing with regard to our basic knowledge of the sequence of humans in the region, the results of the National Park Service excavations led to a reconsideration and reinterpretation of certain aspects of the Brooks River Bluffs phase. And in 1998-1999 a spin-off of this brought excavations by the University of Oregon downstream on the bank of the Naknek River at its tributary Leader Creek.

And so the outlines of human history appeared. [5]

Notes

[1] The radiocarbon method of dating is well publicized as depending on the decay of radioactive carbon atoms at a known rate. To be specific, the radioactive form of carbon (Carbon-14, C-14, or ^{14}C) is formed in the outer atmosphere of Earth as cosmic rays bombard nitrogen atoms. The resulting unstable radioactive carbon-14 constitutes only about one trillionth of all carbon atoms present in the atmosphere. Despite this small proportion of the carbon total, there is enough radioactive carbon in the carbon dioxide absorbed by plants for it to be measured, and as the plants are then consumed by animals a similar level of radioactive carbon comes to be present in all terrestrial forms of life in existence at any one specific time. Operationally, half of the unstable carbon gives off its extra neutron and reverts to nitrogen in about 7,000 years; the trick in providing a radiocarbon age, then, is simply to measure the amount of radioactive carbon remaining, and compare it with the carbon-14 in a modern sample. For this purpose, however, the year 1950 is used as "modern," in order to avoid the extreme radiometric pollution of the atmosphere that resulted from atomic tests; the upshot is that a radiocarbon "age" (often expressed as BP, for Before Present) actually refers to "age before 1950."

There is additional complexity, however. When the radiocarbon method was devised in the mid-twentieth century, it was assumed that the level of radioactive carbon in the earth's atmosphere had always been constant. As radiocarbon ages were calculated on more and more samples, however, some of which had already been dated independently by other means that related them to the modern calendar (samples such as objects from ancient Egypt dated by the Egyptian chronology with its accepted relationship to the modern calendar, and so on) it became more and more clear that there have been fluctuations in radiocarbon "time" that are related to periodic fluctuations in the cosmic bombardment of the earth from the sun. The correction has been to "calibrate" radiocarbon ages by radiocarbon dating individual annual rings of particularly long-lived trees, where a physical count of the rings could provide a date clearly in relation to the known date on which the tree was cut. The result is a calibration curve created by the intersection of radiocarbon ages with the calendar dates derived from tree rings, by means of which the radiocarbon ages are corrected into "calibrated" dates that more closely match those of the modern calendar.

This method is satisfactory for somewhat more than the past 10,000 years — the total span of time being seriously considered in these pages.

Calibrated dates are used here insofar as possible, although in order to relate to ages cited in some of the references given it will often be necessary to mention "radiocarbon age" as distinct from calendar date.

[2] In addition to the original work by Ernest Muller, reported in his Ph.D. dissertation (Muller 1952), further discussions include those of Detterman (1986) and Mann and Peteet (1994). A recent summary of literature dealing with both the glacial and vegetation history of the Naknek River region, with numerous additional references, is by Erickson (2003)

[3] Discussions of the geomorphology of Brooks River and the Ugashik Narrows areas are to be found in Dumond (1981) and Henn (1978) respectively.

[4] This settlement or complex of settlements was referred to during the Russian period as "Severnovskoe seleniya" (i.e., Severnovsk settlements], the people as Severnovskiy. Because the Russian declensional endings make no sense in English, I here use only the root, Severnovsk. Hereafter this word will designate a settlement locale in the aboriginal and early contact period, while I reserve Savonoski for the later settlement established on the lower Naknek River in the twentieth century.

[5] The sequence was first described fairly completely in Dumond (1981), with later research and modifications introduced especially in Dumond (2003).

The More Ancient Past

The Earliest People in Alaska

During the Last Glacial Maximum and the final period of the Pleistocene epoch, the major world concentration of ice was in the ice caps of North America and northern Europe, and the amount of water tied up was enough to lower worldwide sea level by more than 350 feet. This allowed the floor of the shallow continental-shelf sections of the Bering and Chukchi seas to be exposed over more than 1,000 miles (1,600 km.) from north to south, creating a platform of land that united Asia and America. Together with much of Alaska and northeasternmost Asia, this exposed platform formed a region now referred to as Beringia, most of which was not covered by glaciers. Nevertheless, mountains of ice were piled up to the east where the Cordilleran ice sheet of the northern Rocky Mountains met the great

Laurentide ice mass centered on Hudson Bay, and within Alaska ice covered the Alaska Range and the mountains of the Alaska Peninsula.

With the seas shut away from the Bering Strait region for nearly 10,000 years, the climate of interior Beringia was drier and the plant cover included more grass, providing habitat for herds of large grazing animals such as the woolly mammoth, and — enduring longer — herds of bison, horses, and elk or wapiti. In this character Beringia formed an extension of the grassy steppe of northern Asia, and would have been attractive to any human hunters of Asia who were accustomed to prey on such herds — hunters such as are believed to have been present in what is now the southern part of Siberia before

Figure 10 – The North Pacific region.

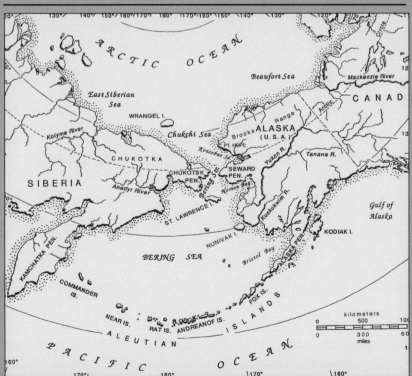

13

20,000 radiocarbon years ago, and on the Kamchatka Peninsula south of the Chukotka province of Russian northeast Asia at least as much as 11,000 radiocarbon years ago (11,000 BC). [1]

That the herds provided an inducement for Siberian hunters to move into what is now Alaska is suggested by the Siberian resemblance of the earliest known Alaskan archaeological remains, ages of which are around 12,000 radiocarbon years, 12,000 BC in true calendar years. This was about 2,000 years earlier than the time of the final flooding of the land bridge that was central Beringia. [2,3] And although the woolly mammoth of the Pleistocene was evidently still present in some parts of Alaska as late as that time,[4] and early people had certainly pursued mammoths as prey in parts of Siberia, there is so far no direct evidence of actual mammoth hunting by the earliest Alaskans. The very few artifacts made of mammoth ivory could equally well be the result either of hunting or of scavenging from older skeletons.

And what manner of people were these earliest known Alaskans? As of now, the earliest of the sites known has produced tiny elongated stone flakes skillfully chipped from stone cores of carefully prepared shape, a form of core that has been called "wedge-shaped," with the derived flakes called "blades" or especially "microblades," because of their small size. As indicated, these are generally similar to contemporary (and also older) artifacts in Siberia, suggesting that they represent the immediate descendants of people moving into what is now Alaska from that region to the west. Whether these Alaskan

Figure 11 – Microblades and wedge-shaped cores of the sort typical of the American Paleoarctic cultural tradition. The scale is 15 cm in length.

microblades were solely intended to be inset into the sides of bone or antler projectile heads, as was the case at the same time in Siberia, or were also used in some other way, is not certain. Nevertheless, a very few bone points with longitudinal slots on the sides presumably intended to hold segments of such small blades have been reported from some Alaskan sites. In general, and as will be seen, this set of Alaskan artifacts and associated debris has been designated the American Paleoarctic tradition. As also noted, the earliest of these Alaskan artifact collections have recently been dated to about 12,000 BC.

By 10,000 BC, however, another people was also present, especially in north Alaska, where two separate groups appear to have been hunting on opposite sides of the Brooks Range. To the south, and possibly also somewhat to the north of the crest of the range, have been found camps of microblade-making descendants of those earliest Paleoarctic people, who still appear to hark fairly directly to Siberia. In several places on the north slope of the range, however, the excavated campsites reveal no evidence of similar microblade making, but instead have yielded well-formed spear or lance points of stone that are extremely similar to artifacts such as have been dated several hundred or even a thousand years earlier in the heartland plains of North America to the south. Most of the radiocarbon ages associated with these artifacts in Alaska run to around 10,000 radiocarbon years ago, or 9500 to 10,000 BC. The most likely explanation for the presence of this apparently new (but ancient) people, although questioned by some archaeologists, is that they mark a movement northward of big-game hunters from interior North America — this after the recession of the major glaciers of the latest Pleistocene had left the way entirely open. For convenience, these sets of artifacts have been called *Paleoindian*. [5]

There is evidence of only the former sort of people — the blade makers — anywhere on the Alaska Peninsula, to which we can now turn.

The Paleoarctic Tradition

Finally, this brings us south to the Alaska Peninsula, where the earliest dated remains are from the narrows between the Upper and Lower Ugashik Lakes, and from a period of a couple of centuries beginning about 9,000 radiocarbon years ago, or around 8000 BC (Figure 12). Remnants of camps of these people, microblade makers comparable to those mentioned above, were revealed simply by good luck, as is so often the case in archaeology.

Ugashik Narrows was visited in 1967, after I heard that local people thought there must be sites there, and their presence was confirmed with a few quick test holes. In 1974, when it seemed desirable to extend work southwestward simply in order to see if the Naknek drainage historical sequence might be duplicated there, we laid out a long trench to cut through and expose what were thought to be former semisubterranean houses represented by surface depressions.

At the very bottom of that trench, a few concentrations of charcoal suggested the one-time presence of campfires, although the actual forms of camps — that is, whether of tents or other shelters — could not be determined. Near the charcoal, artifacts made from flinty stone (chert) included many microblades and the wedge-shaped cores from which they had been chipped or pressed (see Figure 11), plus scraping tools the working ends of which were made by transverse chips struck off by what are technically called "burin blows," and a very few larger stone knives. No organic tools, antler or bone, were preserved. Supported by artifact

15

form and early carbon dates, these remains have been grouped together into what is designated the *Ugashik Narrows* phase of ancient culture, and assigned to the Paleoarctic cultural tradition. [6]

As was indicated earlier, similar remains should be present in areas closer to the Naknek River and the land it drains. One hint that eventually they will be located is provided by a surface find reported by the National Park Service of a blade core and

Figure 12 – Looking east at Ugashik Narrows, the earliest dated site on the Alaska Peninsula. Photo by crew member and late NPS archaeologist Harvey Shields, summer 1974, courtesy of Michele Aubry.

a burin fragment on a southern spur of Mt. Katolinat, south of Iliuk Arm of Naknek Lake. A second and even stronger reason for this expectation came from the nearby mouth of the Kvichak River. In 1974, the Alaska State Archaeologist got in touch with me after receiving reports that wind-eroded sands were exposing artifacts of early people on the floor of an old cannery aircraft runway at a place described as Koggiung. There are, however, several locations called "Koggiung" near the mouth of the Kvichak, and when I finally

located the right place it was the one known to most local people as Graveyard Point (Figure 7). There, only a little work with a trowel in aid of the steady wind uncovered three separate hearth areas, including charcoal that dated at about 8,000 radiocarbon years ago, calibrated to just after 7000 BC. Unlike the site at Ugashik Narrows, the exposures at Graveyard Point were wide enough to make clear that the artifacts were clustered around early campfires. Whether anything like a tent may have once been there couldn't be determined.

Artifacts, again, consisted principally of chert blades and the cores from which they were derived. But on average the blades were somewhat larger than those from Ugashik, as were the cores, and although these cores had a wedge-like edge chipped at the base (presumably to allow them to be shoved into some kind of vise, possibly a split log, while blades were pressed off), they were considerably fatter than those from Ugashik. There were also a few knife-like artifacts. The collection as a whole was finally designated the *Koggiung* phase of culture.[7] I admit my first impulse was to call it the Graveyard phase, but I decided to hold that name for what seemed a better purpose, as will be indicated in the succeeding section.

What were these Paleoarctic people doing on the Alaska Peninsula? Although neither of these sites yielded preserved animal remains, evidence elsewhere in Alaska has suggested that people of that period were hunters of terrestrial game — presumably caribou on the peninsula, but farther north and somewhat earlier the game had included an extinct form of bison, as well as elk or wapiti. As noted before, Ugashik Narrows was then, and remains, an active crossing for land animals of all sorts, and presumably the situation was comparable at Graveyard Point with a crossing of the ancestral Kvichak River, although the early form of the landscape is not so clearly understood there.

The fairly subtle changes in artifacts that can be discerned between the Narrows and the Koggiung phases are common to the same period elsewhere in Alaska — 9,000 to 8,000 radiocarbon years ago. Further, by the time of the Koggiung phase at about 7000 BC, blade-making people had expanded from the Alaska mainland southeastward through the coastal panhandle, with presumed relatives appearing on the Queen Charlotte Islands of British Columbia and farther south. A few of their sites provide evidence of intensive use of coastal resources — shellfish and some fish. And by the same time, blade-making people were present in the Fox Islands of the eastern Aleutians, where their subsistence was certainly from the sea, for on the islands there was no significant alternative.

The Northern Archaic Tradition

A similar hunting way of life was apparently followed during the next major cultural stage as seen both on the Alaska Peninsula and in interior Alaska to the north. Hence there is little surprise that these later remains are often found on exactly those sites that yielded artifacts of the Paleoarctic predecessors; this is the case at Ugashik Narrows, at Graveyard Point and elsewhere (Figure 15). In general, this stage fell somewhere around 5000 BC to 2500 BC, and the people were hunting animals of purely modern form. Such was the case in the expanding forests of the Alaskan interior as well as on the treeless Alaska Peninsula, where one must suppose that, like the Narrows and Koggiung phase folk before them, these people continued to be hunters of contemporary herd animals — caribou.

With the advent of this second cultural tradition, referred to generally as *Northern Archaic*, despite the maintenance of a roughly similar way of life there was a radical change in the character of the artifacts. Now, the most common objects were rather crudely made stone points,

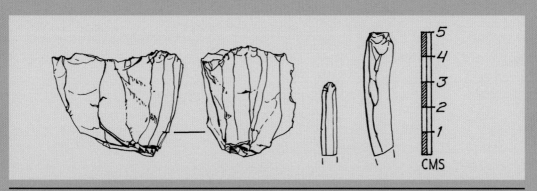

Figure 13 – A core and blades typical of the easternmost Aleutian Islands about 9,000 years ago.

Figure 14 – Two unidentified Koggiung village men throwing darts with their throwing boards, circa 1915. The atlatl contests were frequent evening entertainment for the Diamond J cannery men. The atlatl was used to increase the arm leverage, thereby enhancing the force with which the dart would impact the target. Photo courtesy of Mr. and Mrs. Matt Davey.

often of basalt, usually with broad notches from the corner or side for binding them to the end of a shaft. The size, weight, and width across the stem or between the notches of these points suggest that they were too large for arrows, and thus tipped heavier darts probably used with the spear thrower or *atlatl* (a pre-Spanish word from Mexico adopted by many archaeologists, see Figure 14). There were also

varieties of scraping tools, and in a few cases in some areas — but not on the peninsula — notched pebbles that may have been parts of fishing gear. Some Alaskan sites, although possibly a minority, also included blades reminiscent of those of the Paleoarctic peoples, but broader and cruder and taken from cores that were much less carefully prepared than had been the case earlier.

The characteristic projectile points are known from both Ugashik Narrows and Graveyard Point, where they have been dated to sometime around 3700 BC. The presence of blades together with these crude stone points is clear at Ugashik Narrows, in what is designated the Ugashik Knoll phase. Similar blades were probably also used in the same period at Graveyard Point, although when that site was studied much erosion had already removed the sands to a point well below the levels of most campsites of comparable Northern Archaic people. Indeed, although in excavations beside the eroding Graveyard Point runway we were able to locate appropriate former ground surfaces laden with chips, crude scraping tools, and charcoal which produced radiocarbon ages appropriate to the Northern Archaic tradition, we actually found none of the characteristic projectile points. For these we could rely only on photographs of artifacts that had led the State Archaeologist to alert us to the site, except for the generosity of Cal Martin and his young son Danny. Fishermen from Anchorage, they were pleased to donate some characteristic Northern Archaic artifacts they had found on the eroding runway a

Figure 15 – Recent NPS archaeological investigations at Kukaklek Lake have found evidence of Northern Archaic camps at the same location as their Paleoarctic predecessors. Photo by Dale Vinson 1999.

few weeks before, which we designated the *Graveyard* phase. What I had called the Koggiung phase had included no projectile points, so to satisfy a fit of whimsy, I rescued Graveyard as the name of the later phase especially so I could refer to the projectiles as "Graveyard points." [8]

In later stages of the Northern Archaic tradition, there was a tendency for the projectile points to become more elongated, and less strongly notched and stemmed. Farther north in the Alaska interior this development is reported at about 3000 BC, and, as we shall see, not many centuries after that time signs of apparently the same appeared within the Naknek

drainage region itself, on what was then the bank of Brooks River near its mouth.

But this introduces the subject to be pursued in the following sections, as present information regarding the cultural progression specifically along the course of the Naknek drainage system will be outlined. The sequence itself was diagrammed in Figure 6, which gives the technical terms applied. It also shows the progression of tephras or volcanic ash deposits that were found to punctuate the sequence, which in some cases may signal eruptions that had important effects on the humans who lived there.

Figure 16 – Stone projectile points of the Northern Archaic tradition present on the northern Alaska Peninsula. Scale 20 cm in length.

The Kittiwick Period

As a blow against simplicity, in the upper Naknek drainage region the period before 2000 BC is represented not by artifacts that appear to have derived from a single group of people, but rather by sets of artifacts from two groups, quite evidently different from one another. Although a few artifacts probably pertaining to them have been recorded near the head of Brooks River on Brooks Lake, the major campsites during this period — 3000 to 2000 BC — were scattered on the two sides of what at the time was the very mouth of Brooks River, on what are now wooded ridges well back from the present Naknek Lake shore. These ridges are marked in Figure 17 as areas XMK-041

and XMK-032, their crests now about 6 meters (20 feet) above the level of the modern lake. One must presume that these two groups, each distinct from the other in terms of territorial focus in Alaska generally, were present at Brooks River only occasionally, possibly haphazardly, and almost certainly were not together there in the same year and possibly not even in the same decade.

As I said before, after the concentrated season of 1963 at Brooks River, I was convinced there was no trace of human campsites to be found below volcanic ash G, which underlay all the camps of the Brooks River Gravels people. But only the following year, 1964, I was proved wrong.

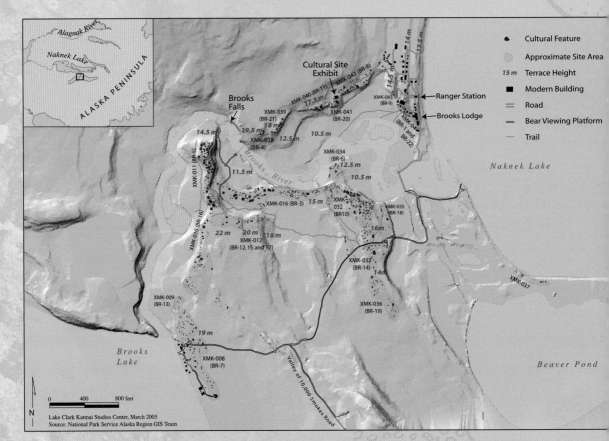

Figure 17 – Archaeological sites and the river and lake terraces around Brooks River.

THE MORE ANCIENT PAST – Earliest Known People at Brooks River: The Kittiwick Period

That season the major Oregon crew of six people was set to work on the Shelikof Strait coast of Katmai National Monument with effort centered at Kukak Bay. Meanwhile, with one young assistant I was back at Brooks River to finish up some odds and ends that were still hanging. While in the midst of minor excavations on one of those ridges (XMK-032 or BR10) that had formed near what had been the mouth of the river around 3000 BC, I took a chartered flight of inspection to the camp at Kukak Bay. When I got back after a day or two, my assistant told me — without apparently realizing the significance — that he had found occupation debris below the yellow ash G. He was right and I was flabbergasted, and we shortly repeated the stunt across the river (at XMK-041 or BR20). And so were found the two, roughly contemporary but distinct, Brooks River Strand and Brooks River Beachridge phases.

Brooks River Strand Phase –

Slightly the earlier of the two, as now dated, were camps of the *Brooks River Strand* phase, with three radiocarbon ages spanning from 4400 to 3900 years, calibrated to indicate dates somewhere between 3200 and 2400 BC. The artifacts from these camps were completely unlike those of any occupations mentioned so far, in that they included large lance-like points of polished slate as well as stemmed stone points made by chipping, and in the largest of the campsites included broken vessels of stone that had evidently been used as oil lamps. The initial find below ash G, for which there were

no surface signs, led in 1964 and 1965 to a program of blind test-pitting along terraces and beach ridges that had no visible surface indications and that had formed before the deposit of ash G nearly 4,000 years ago. In one of these, a small habitation was represented by a floor roughly tear-drop shaped

Figure 18 – Finding the earliest sites required test pits in the woods and well away from the present river.

and heavily stained with charcoal, excavated about six inches into the contemporaneous ground, and covered with smashed mammal bone including the very deteriorated remnant of what is thought to have been a caribou skull. The floor yielded a long and impressive slate lance blade, a chipped stone point, and a radiocarbon age of 4430 ± 110, possibly somewhat before 3000 BC in calendar years. This presumably was the floor of a tent of some kind.

By the time this was excavated (in 1965) similar and contemporary artifacts had been found by archaeologists both on the Alaska Peninsula coast of Shelikof Strait

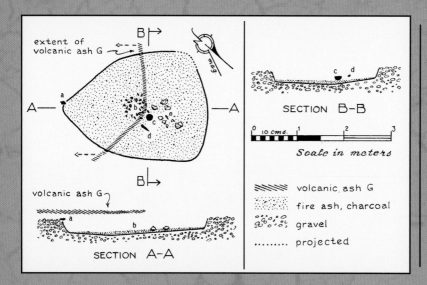

Figure 19 – The charcoal-stained tent floor of the Brooks River Strand phase. Artifacts included (a) a chipped stone projectile point, (b) a mass of stone chips, (c) decomposed bone, apparently what was left of part of a caribou skull, (d) a long polished slade lance blade, and (e) a crudely chipped implement almost without form, and of unknown use.

and on Kodiak Island. The conclusion, easily enough, is that these at Brooks River were Pacific coastal people who had crossed the Aleutian Range of mountains in search of caribou. The use of the finely polished slate implements aligns them with people of the Pacific coast of this time, and their use of oil-burning lamps marks them as a coastal people who were accustomed to hunting sea mammals.

Nevertheless, the most impressive find of the Strand phase occurred later and involved even more blind luck than when we found the small habitation. In 1967 there were four of us at Brooks River, this time to excavate houses that might serve as National Park Service displays. Located on the same old beach of Naknek Lake that had yielded the tent floor just described, a Camp phase house — large, with well-defined edges, a sunken entrance tunnel, and convenient to the tourist facilities at Brooks Lodge — was

quickly selected by National Park Service people as the best exhibit candidate. But while we were cleaning it up so it could be consolidated, it rained.

In 1967 torrential rains at Fairbanks caused the Chena River to flood and wash out the Alaska Centennial Exposition that was going on at the time. In the same days, Brooks River had downpours, including three inches in a single night. Water in the excavated house began to rise. It was obvious that if the house were to serve as an exhibit, some serious engineering measures would have to forestall future flooding. This meant a deep trench upslope of the house, connecting to others leading around it in which a line of perforated pipe could drain the water well down the hill toward the river.

It was this trench, dug deeper than the house and its sunken entryway and at least a couple of feet into the very

THE MORE ANCIENT PAST – Earliest Known People at Brooks River: The Kittiwick Period

compacted gravel surface of the ancient beach below, that exposed a series of campfires, living surfaces yielding slate blades, chipped stone implements, fragments of flat oil-burning lamps, and a radiocarbon age of 3900 ± 100 years, or about 2500 BC. This capped the serendipitous finds of the Strand phase. In time, the phase took its place as clearly a northerly outlier of what has been called the Kodiak tradition, [10] centered on the northern Gulf of Alaska and outside of the geographic limits of the present account.

Brooks River Beachridge Phase –

The second group of things below volcanic ash G, overlapping in time with the Strand phase, has been designated the *Brooks River Beachridge* phase, with a pair of radiocarbon ages at about 3,800 and 4,000 years, or between about 2900 and 2300 BC. The collections are small in number of artifacts — chipped stone points of generalized leaf shape and small scraping tools of chipped stone. Smashed mammal bone, probably from caribou limb bones, was plentiful in the small camps, but so fragmented that positive identification of species is impossible. Comparing these collections with those from elsewhere in Alaska, especially

0 1 2 3 4 5 6 7 8 9 10 11 12 13 14 15 16 17 18 19 20

Figure 20 – Artifacts of the Brooks River Strand phase. At the far left is the lance blade from the tent floor (Figure 19) with four more polished slate artifacts to the right of it. The three light-colored objects (center and top center) are artifacts of chipped stone. To the right is a flat, oil-burning lamp of stone, found broken in three pieces. The scale is 20 cm.

northward and toward the interior, suggests that these people were probably descendants of somewhat earlier people similar to those of the Ugashik Knoll and Graveyard phases. That is, we concluded they were people related primarily to those of the Alaska interior, hunters of terrestrial animals, especially caribou, who represented a late stage of the Northern Archaic tradition.

It is not impossible given the dating that the two groups — Strand and Beachridge — were actually completely separated in time, and that the presence at Brooks River of the latter group really postdated that of people of the Strand phase. But the remains of both groups are so thin and scattered in the Brooks River area, and the radiocarbon evidence so overlapping, that this cannot be demonstrated. And in terms of the basic stratigraphy, both appeared between the same layers of early volcanic ash of the many such encountered in the area — all sites covered by what is designated volcanic ash G, and all above volcanic ash H or I. The safest conclusion is that the groups represented two different peoples who during some of the same centuries made a desultory use especially of the mouth of Brooks River as an attractive campsite while engaged in hunting caribou.

It is the placement of the camps that suggests that focus on hunting, bespeaking an apparent lack of interest in the overall course of an even shorter river than that of today — an absence of any interest such as would be expected of people who were drawn to the river for fishing.

Interestingly, at that former river mouth the remains of the Strand-phase people were found only on the north side, whereas those of the Beachridge people were found on the south. But whatever that may signify, the collections of the two groups were not separated perfectly, for in small camps of what were considered the Brooks River Strand phase there were a few chipped implements with notched sides that would have seemed more at home in the Beachridge phase. In any event, for now the safest practical policy for the archaeologist has been to take the river as the practical dividing line.

The Gomer Period

The designation of this period also involved a bit of humor. The so-called Gomer Hole on Brooks River is well known to fishermen, and was reportedly named for a former Fish and Wildlife employee with the first name of Gomer who had a predilection for fishing there. During our first season at Brooks River, however, when we cheechakos asked "What's a gomer?" one joker told us that "a gomer is a little invisible guy that puts water in hipboots and tangles fishing line and generally raises heck." After we returned from the first season at Brooks River we were told by archaeologists experienced in the north that the limited collection of very small artifacts we were deciding to call the Brooks River Gravels phase resembled what some of them called the Arctic Small Tool tradition. In much of our second season we kept turning up similar miniature tools clearly mixed into later

THE MORE ANCIENT PAST – First Heavy Use of the River: The Gomer Period

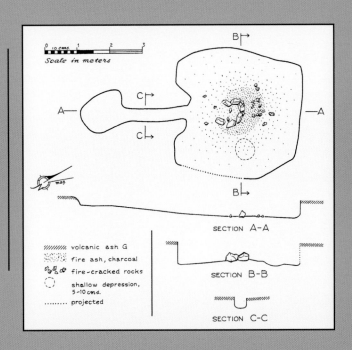

Figure 21 – Plan and cross-sections of a semisubterranean house of the Brooks River Gravels phase, the first such house that we were able to excavate completely. This particular floor was not dated by carbon, but similar houses produced ages of about 3,600 to 3,100 radiocarbon years, equivalent to calendar dates of around 2000 to 1300 BC.

collections, unable to locate a real Gravels phase deposit; it was as though we were chasing pixies, rather than real people. So we began to refer to them as Gomers, the magical Little People. The name stuck.

It was the very end of the second season's work at Brooks River before we isolated hearths and occupation floors pertaining to the phase. But the next four seasons of excavation there made the earlier difficulty seem astounding. By then we knew that constructed houses of Gravels phase people were to be found on almost every terrace of Brooks River that was in existence during the period of their use of the river, and that such houses occurred beneath almost every other set of occupation remains along the river. When our basic work had been completed we concluded from the evidence that at least 100 such houses were in existence along the

river, and that very possibly the number was double that, if not even higher. [11] Why did it take so long to find them? It was because most of their sites lie well back from the modern river channel, and are now hidden in the expanding spruce forest — where, it seemed, no archaeologist with an undisturbed mind would think to dig.

What were these people up to? Whatever else they may have done, they were certainly there to fish. Although some smashed mammal bone was found (not identifiable to genus or species), showing that large animals such as caribou were also a focus, the scatter of houses along the former river course makes it clear that the river itself was their main interest. To clinch the argument, in 1973 a trio of us returned to Brooks River to take more floor samples from houses of the phase. These yielded salmonid teeth, possibly large trout but much more likely those of migrating salmon; this would indicate occupation in the summer or fall.

The houses, roughly square and about 12 to 13 feet on a side, were uniformly excavated from eight to 20 inches into the contemporary surface, cutting through volcanic ash G, which had then been in the surface sod. And spots of the distinctive yellow ash G scattered over the floors suggested that at least some sod was used on roofs, all of which would seem to suggest that the habitations were suitable for wintertime occupancy. Whatever the actual season of use, these houses were entered from the outside ground surface along sloping passages. Interestingly, no clear evidence of postholes toward the center of the floors was recovered, the

only unmistakable case of posts being a pair of slanting holes in one edge of one house. It is entirely possible that the roofs were constructed simply by flexible poles thrust lightly into the ground around the house edge, their tops then bound together over the center of the floor. Nevertheless, toward the centers of the floors was charcoal, usually surrounding a box-like arrangement of rocks that enclosed little if any charcoal, but had piles of small fire-cracked rocks alongside. These boxes were probably frames to support the edges of green animal hides, to be filled with water and used with heated rocks in the stone-boiling of fish or other foods.

Numerous radiocarbon ages range from about 3,600 to 3,100 years, which

0 1 2 3 4 5 6 7 8 9 10 11 12 13 14 15 16 17 18 19 20

Figure 22 – Artifacts of the Brooks River Gravels phase. The object at the upper right is an adze blade of basalt, with a polished bit; below it to the right is a squared, chipped stone knife; to the immediate left of which is a burin or grooving tool. In the upper center, to the left of the adze blade are two microblades. On the left is a large chipped-stone knife, and to the immediate lower right of it are three well-made stone scrapers. There are nine projectile blades of various sizes and shapes, two are on the far right, three are below and to the left of the adze blade, and four are in the upper left. The scale is 20 cm.

calibrate to about 2000 to 1300 BC. And who were these people? Their artifacts, which stand out dramatically from those of all other phases, consist of very small and delicate leaf-shaped or narrowly elongated chipped points of fine flinty rock. From the size and conformation these must certainly have been tips for arrows, a departure from the earlier and larger projectile blades that must have been used as thrusting spears or thrown with a spear thrower. In addition, there were very delicate and well made scraping tools; small stone adze blades with polished bits; a few larger chipped knives; small grooving tools ("burins") made either by chipping or by polishing the edge of a small stone otherwise chipped to a shape similar to the arrow points; and a few microblades.

All of these tie the people to the *Arctic Small Tool* tradition, a large unit that includes comparable early remains spread all the way from Bering Strait and north Alaska (where they are known as the *Denbigh Flint* complex) around the top of America to Greenland. Campsites of these Denbigh people are especially plentiful in the Brooks Range of north Alaska, where they were located evidently to intercept migrating herds of caribou. Although a few of the sites there suggest lakeside or small river fishing, none is close to rivers with major runs of anadromous fish such as the salmon that run into the Naknek and other rivers emptying into the Bering Sea. For the most part, the dates for these northern sites, from Alaska eastward to Greenland, show beginning radiocarbon ages of about 4,500 to 4,200 years ago (3300 - 2800 BC). The Denbigh Flint complex generally thrived in north Alaska only until about 3,600 radiocarbon years ago (2000 BC), but in northernmost Canada descendant Arctic Small Tool people (called Dorset) can be recognized at or not long after 1000 BC, and were present until after 1000 radiocarbon years ago, or AD 900.

Interestingly also, constructed houses of this Brooks River sort are virtually nonexistent in other Arctic Small Tool tradition sites throughout the entire Alaskan area, where camps of Small Tool people are generally thought to have involved surface tents. A northern exception is at a site on the Kobuk River, at the southwest corner of the Brooks Range, where a habitation floor is interpreted as having been related to some kind of tent-like structure excavated somewhat into the ground; some others of the sort may also be present in the Brooks Range, but the evidence is not definitive. On the Bering Sea side of the Alaska Peninsula, however, the houses were not confined to Brooks River, for a site pertaining to people using an apparently similar house is recorded at Ugashik Narrows from around 2300 BC, and another on the Kvichak River below the outlet of Iliamna Lake is dated about 400 years later. [12]

A few scattered artifacts suggestive of the Brooks River Gravels phase of the Arctic Small Tool tradition are known from the Pacific coast of the Alaska Peninsula and on Kodiak Island and Cook Inlet, but here they are mixed with artifacts of what were basically people of a different and more obviously coastal way of life. A much more clearly related Small Tool site has been found on Kachemak Bay, off of Cook Inlet, where the small campsite is dated around 2700 BC. [13] This certainly must have represented a southern incursion by Small Tool people, but with that event any such incursion seems to have stopped. There is no more evidence to be had of their presence in the region south and east of the Aleutian Range.

The specific origin of these folk appears most likely to have lain in Siberia, where people of the Neolithic era made use of a highly similar range of artifacts, although they also were using pottery, which is not reported at this time from Alaska, and thus far none of their sites have been identified near Bering Strait. The earliest dated Alaskan Small Tool site is on the Seward Peninsula, where it is apparently not later than about 3500 BC and could be earlier. The implication of the evidence appears to be that these people had moved in from Siberia to hunt within the far northern tundra zone near the coast, where some of them then turned to sea mammal hunting and perhaps to occasional lake fishing.[14] In terms of what is now known, the Gravels-phase houses at Brooks River and the related sites at Ugashik Narrows and the Kvichak River, all located on watercourses with substantial salmon runs, appear to be from later stages of the Arctic Small Tool tradition — involving people who had become adapted to fish runs and lived in a fashion somewhat more settled or sedentary than did their earlier northern relatives.

Whatever the development toward increasingly sedentary settlements, the southern Arctic Small Tool people of the Brooks River Gravels phase, like most of their relatives farther north, simply vanished after a time. To the extent that archaeology enables one to judge, their disappearance was relatively sudden, and in the Naknek region was evidently succeeded by a break in use of the area by humans. There, the end of the Gravels phase and of the Arctic Small Tool tradition came at about 3100 radiocarbon years ago, or perhaps 1300 BC. Although the close of the Small Tool period has been placed as early as 2000 BC in some areas of north Alaska, and although attempts have been made to see a direct transition there to later human occupants, the success of these intellectual efforts is somewhat doubtful. Yet scattered remnants of Small Tool people may have continued for a time in the eastern Brooks Range, and in northern Canada and Greenland descendant Small Tool folk were present an additional millennium before their development into the people of Dorset culture.

What could have happened in Alaska in general and the Naknek region in particular? The most obvious possible explanation is that the subsistence base of the people collapsed. With their heavy reliance on caribou wherever they lived, a major slump in caribou populations would certainly have caused serious problems, and possibly famines. In the upper Naknek River drainage area there are also indications of volcanic eruptions. At Brooks River, specifically, volcanic ash F is a thick deposit of ash-like pumice that overlies all Gravels phase occupation, and has been suggested to have resulted from massive eruptions occurring as far southwest along the Alaska Peninsula as Aniakchak Volcano, located not far east of Port Heiden. A major eruption in that particular region, if sufficient to blanket much of the peninsula, could well have essentially eliminated the Alaska Peninsula caribou herd, which at least in modern days collects to calve around Port Heiden. The second subsistence resource here, of course, is fish. With recent indications from the analysis of lake cores that certain periods in southern Alaska have seen declines in fish runs amounting almost to cessation, any such event coinciding even partly with large volcanic eruptions at the crucial time could have spelled, of itself, the end of the Gravels phase population in the region. [15]

The Brooks River Period

The designation of this period was chosen simply because the majority of the cultural remains thus far known are from portions of the Naknek drainage system above the major course of the Naknek River itself. The few sites of the period recorded on the upper portions of the Naknek River are above the mouth of Smelt Creek. And although there are other sites located above Naknek Lake near the confluence of the outlet of Lake Grosvenor and the Savonoski River, occupations of this time were especially heavy at Brooks River.

Remains of all three cultural phases that fall into this period were encountered during the first two seasons of work in the Naknek region, and were explored much more fully during four subsequent summers. All are clearly related to one another

Figure 23 – Excavations in progress on the bank of the Naknek River at the Smelt Creek site, 1973.

in a sequential fashion and have been recognized as belonging to a geographically broad cultural division that has been termed the Norton tradition. The name in this case was drawn from the related Norton culture first reported from Norton Bay at the end of the 1940s, although related to finds made earlier at Point Hope and to others made not long afterward near the northern coast a short distance east of the Alaska boundary with Canada. [16]

The first of these phases encountered in our excavations was the middle one, the Brooks River Weir phase, exposed in 1960. The year 1961 brought initial excavations at the major Smelt Creek site on the middle Naknek River, excavations both expanded and corrected in 1973. In both 1961 and 1965 traces of the Smelt Creek phase were also recorded at Brooks River, and in 1961 and 1963 major excavations along the same river were in sites of the Falls phase, which in turn was also recorded in the upper Naknek River in 1974.

Sites affiliated with the Norton tradition depart from those of the preceding period of the Arctic Small Tool tradition in several distinctive ways. In the first place, with the exception of a locality only a few miles within northwesternmost Canada, Norton tradition sites are limited to Alaska alone, in an area stretching around the entire northern and western coast to the Alaska Peninsula on the south. Pottery is present in most of these sites, without doubt a borrowing from contemporary ceramic use in northeastern Siberia. So also in most sites are stone vessels used as lamps to burn sea mammal oil. Lip ornaments, or labrets, to be inserted through a perforation in the lower lip, made their plentiful appearance. Constructed houses were widespread, excavated well into the contemporary ground surface, evidently roofed with some sod, entered generally by a sloping passageway, and with a fireplace toward the center of the floor. Groups of these houses are common on the coast, in contrast to more ephemeral Norton campsites in some interior locations — except, that is, in Norton-related sites along salmon streams emptying into the Bering Sea, where houses may be extensive. Indeed, the majority of sites are to be found south of the Seward Peninsula, underscoring a developed interest in harvesting massive fish runs, while the taking of sea mammals along the coast was also practiced. Compared to most representatives of the Arctic Small Tool period, increases in sedentariness and in attention both to seacoasts and salmon streams are unmistakable.

Smelt Creek Phase –

In northwestern Alaska and at Norton Bay, Norton culture remains are commonly dated at or slightly before 500 BC. On the upper Naknek River the beginning of the earliest of the three related historical units, the Smelt Creek phase, has been dated at about 2,300 radiocarbon years ago, perhaps 400 BC, and at Ugashik Narrows possibly a century later —

altogether an indication of the arrival of Norton people from farther north. Thus, at Brooks River and apparently in the Naknek region generally, there was a major period between the disappearance of Arctic Small Tool folk and the arrival of Norton people in which there were apparently no human occupants — a period that must have lasted for most of a millennium, from 1300 or possibly 1200 BC to 400 BC. Why? At this point, nobody knows, although as indicated earlier this break in occupation coincides with at least two volcanic eruptions, one of which according to the depth of volcanic ash at Brooks River must have been substantial, and may have had an impact on much of the Alaska Peninsula. [17]

The distinction between the earliest Norton-related phase and the two later ones that are closely allied to it is based partly on radiocarbon ages, but also depends on observable features among the plentiful pottery, the chipped stone projectile points, the chipped knife blades, and the polished slate. Of these, slate artifacts begin to be moderately plentiful in the second of the phases, the Brooks River Weir phase, and in the final Brooks River Falls phase have almost completely displaced earlier side-hafted knife blades of chipped stone. It must be emphasized, however, that the transitions from one to the other of the phases are gradual in all of these dimensions.

Figure 24 – Stone artifacts of the Brooks River period, Smelt Creek through Brooks River Falls phases. Top left side, adze blade with polished bit, ulu blade (top right) and lance blade of polished slate (top center). Center area, eight chipped-stone projectile points of various sizes. Lower right, a small lip ornament or labret of jet. Bottom, five asymmetrical knives or side blades of chipped stone. Scale is 15 cm.

Figure 25 – Reconstructed pots of the Brooks River period. Left, Smelt Creek phase; right, Brooks River Weir phase.

For example, the Smelt Creek phase is especially characterized by pottery with inclusions ("temper") [18] of hair or other fiber, appearing in vessels of a specific shape in which the mouths of relatively tall cooking pots or jars are contracted inward, and which on the outside exhibit small surface impressions such as are made on waffles by the waffle iron ("check-stamped"). It also includes very plentiful chipped knife blades to be side-hafted in a wooden or bone handle ("side blades"), and many chipped stone projectile points ("end blades") very often of basalt, with long and contracting bases, although there are a number of small leaf-shaped points highly reminiscent of those of the earlier Brooks River Gravels phase. And there are small chipped-stone adze blades with polished cutting edges that are indistin-guishable from those of the Gravels phase, as are a few polished grooving implements. These latter two classes, however, appear to be the only ones in the phase in which stone artifacts were finished by grinding. In addition to midden or trash deposits, only a single small house of the phase has been excavated: roughly oblong but less than 10 feet in length, with a more or less central hearth and an apparent entry as a sunken spot at one corner. It may actually have been the base of a tent structure of some kind. From calibrated radiocarbon ages, the phase can be dated between about 400 or 300 BC and AD 1.

Brooks River Weir Phase –

The second local division of the Norton tradition in the Brooks River period, the Brooks River Weir phase, is marked by erect-rimmed, cylindrical-shaped pottery, often without visible surface decoration, but also often with check-stamped impressions about twice the size of those of the previous phase. Comparable projectile end blades tend to be somewhat smaller, and to have a constricting base area that is shorter in proportion to total length than was the case previously, or may have a set-off stem leading to decidedly rounded shoulders. Polished slate knives for side-hafting as ulus appear, as do a few flat, double-edged knives or lance blades of polished slate. Chipped side blades, however, continue, although with overall shapes that depart from those of the Smelt Creek phase. The phase can be dated to the period from about AD 1 to AD 550 or 600.

My present impression is that in terms of artifact style the phase lasted somewhat longer than the other two divisions of the Brooks River period, and with further analysis it may come to be subdivided.

A series of houses or partial houses has been excavated. All appear to have been rather slight structures in terms of framework (remains of which were generally not found), the floors excavated 6 inches to a foot or more into the contemporary ground surface. These were generally square or squarish, up to about 15 feet across, and probably were usually entered by a short sloping passageway. Only one was actually excavated to completeness in early work at Brooks River, although work by the National Park Service revealed apparent houses of the same sort not far from that one.[19] Indeed, in form these were clearly similar to those of the much earlier Brooks River Gravels phase.

Brooks River Falls Phase –

In the third, or Brooks River Falls, phase, the overall shape of the Weir phase pottery continued, although it was generally not decorated with check-stamped (or any other) impressions, was thicker, and near the end of the phase had a noticeable increase in inclusions ("temper") of small gravel somewhat at the expense of the former fiber. Small chipped-stone end blades now tended to have pronounced barbs, flat lance blades or double-edged knives of polished slate increased, and the single-edged knife or ulu of polished slate had almost completely replaced the earlier chipped side blades.

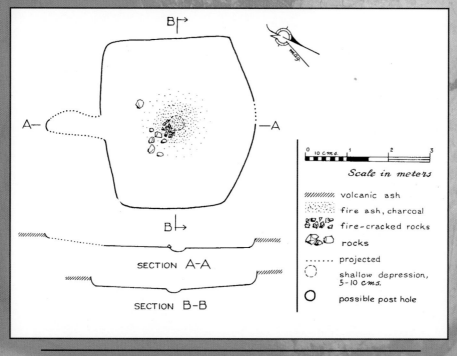

Figure 26 – Plan and sections of a house of the Brooks River Weir phase. Charcoal on this floor dated to about AD 100.

Unfortunately, no recognizable houses where floors could be fully cleared were encountered in excavations. In one trench, a fireplace ringed by flagstones appeared within some four feet of an aboriginal cut that was probably the edge of a semisubterranean house, but the surrounding matrix was a midden area that had been so disturbed by miscellaneous ancient digging and other activities that house edges were impossible to follow. Nevertheless, the relationship suggested that Falls phase houses were in essence the same as those of the preceding Weir phase. The hearth was dated by radiocarbon at about 1300 years ago, calibrated at AD 700 to 750. The phase as a whole is dated to the period of about AD 600 to 1000.

Discussion: The Brooks River Period of the Naknek Region –

As indicated earlier, sites of the phases of the Brooks River period are found in various places between the portion of the Naknek drainage area that is above Naknek Lake (i.e., on Brooks and Savonoski rivers) and segments of the Naknek River above the mouth of Smelt Creek, although some scattered artifacts apparently related to the phases have been picked up at a few places downstream. That the center of gravity was located in the upper course of the drainage is quite in keeping with the indications from elsewhere that Norton tradition people around the Bering Sea had a strong interest in systematic fishing, an indication supported in both the Smelt Creek and Brooks River Falls phases by

finds of notched pebbles interpreted as fish net sinkers. Unfortunately, no faunal remains survived in any site of the Brooks River period, a situation that can be at least partly explained by the acidity of the local soils and the absence of permanently frozen deposits, hence the conclusion that fishing was a major activity must be inferred less directly.

However, an absence of Norton tradition sites from the lower river and coastline is very possibly more related to the progressive tidal erosion of the banks in that area than to the habits of the people of the Brooks River period. Farther to the north around the Bering Sea, Norton-related sites have yielded small toggling harpoon heads of bone — that is, heads attached to a line, but designed to come loose from the harpoon shaft and twist sideways to hold after an animal is struck with it.

Figure 27 – Small decorated stone vessel of the Brooks River Weir phase. The face in relief on the front shows the wearing of a pair of ornaments (labrets) below the lower lip. Maximum width is about 4 inches (10 cm).

These were evidently used to hunt the smaller sea mammals such as seals, and Norton-related remains are common on the Walrus Islands of outer Bristol Bay. At one site north of Bering Strait the finds also included large harpoon heads thought suitable for the taking of whales. [20]

But despite the absence of any known site on the coast near Naknek, evidence exists that these people were attracted to the sea-mammal-rich southeast coast of the peninsula on the Gulf of Alaska. There, a site with the characteristic pottery and a few other artifacts of the Brooks River Weir phase is dated at AD 300 to 400; and after about AD 600 square semisubterranean houses have produced substantial amounts of distinctive Falls phase pottery, chipped and barbed Falls phase end blades, and other artifacts, but they are parts of tool collections that also include implements known from the quite different local Pacific coastal culture of earlier centuries. Although the differences between collections from the two sides of the peninsula dating to the first millennium AD are great enough that one cannot well conclude that there were Weir or Falls phase settlements on the Pacific coast, the character of many artifacts certainly suggests that there was communication across the peninsula, and also the likelihood that some immigrants from the Naknek region had crossed the Aleutian Range to join their Pacific Coast contemporaries. In addition, some sites probably related to these of the Naknek-area phases of the late Brooks River period have been reported from the Bering Sea coast near the mouth of the

Ugashik River to the southwest, although they have been little explored. [21]

The Naknek Period

The changes discernible between the material objects of the Gomer period and those of the succeeding Brooks River period were outlined above, and although there were certain classes of implements that evidently continued from the earlier to the later period (implements such as the small bipointed projectile blades, and the small adze blades with polished bits), the elapsed time between the two may have approached a thousand years. On the other hand, the changes in artifact form between the material culture of the Brooks River period and that of the succeeding Naknek period were equally as great, yet the changes came about apparently suddenly and without any real indication that the periods were separated by any significant interval of abandonment.

Like the Brooks River period, this Naknek period embodies three sequential phases — the Brooks River Camp, the Brooks River Bluffs, and the Pavik phases. The three together I have suggested to be part of the widespread Thule tradition, a continent-wide cultural stream that had its beginning in the Bering Strait region and then expanded both northeast and southeast from there. The name is taken from that applied to the archaeological culture of those people who in the early second millennium AD moved across northernmost North America from Alaska to Greenland, and who exemplified the prototypical culture of essentially all the late prehistoric coastal people of mainland

Alaska. [22] The first two of these phases, the Camp and Bluffs, preceded the arrival of Europeans in the area. The third, the Pavik phase, is dated from the beginning of contact with Russians and the appearance of European and other foreign trade items, and lasts until about the time of the purchase of Alaska by the United States and the beginnings of the commercial fishing industry late in the nineteenth century. Unlike the phases of the Brooks River period, which flowed from one to the other in apparently undisturbed evolution, each of the three phases of the Naknek period appears to some extent to have involved the arrival of a new people in the Naknek region.

Brooks River Camp Phase –

Around the Bering Sea as a whole, the changes reflected in the advent of the Naknek period included the widespread appearance of new, polished-slate-using cultures that replaced phases of the earlier Norton tradition. In the Naknek region the Brooks River Camp phase initiated this sharp break with the immediately preceding Falls phase in pervasive ways. In pottery, the tempering material now showed almost no fiber, but was consistently small-to-medium-sized gravel, while the shape changed from cylinder to more of a globe, with constricted and more-or-less narrow base matched at the top by an inward tapering rim, although sometimes flaring at the very lip. The oil-burning stone lamps of the Brooks River period were suddenly replaced by saucer-shaped lamps of clay, fired lightly or sometimes not fired at all. Polished slate almost completely replaced chipped stone for all finished implements, including for the first time small polished slate points that could be inserted as tips in either arrowheads or toggling harpoon heads made of bone or antler. Lance blades of polished slate often departed from the flatter slate implements of earlier times by the introduction of a longitudinal and central rib, narrowed stem, and barbs. Large polished stone adze blades now included some with grooves across the outer face to allow them to be lashed directly to wooden hafts ("splitting adze").

Houses, a number of which have been

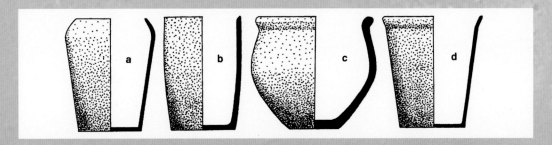

Figure 28 – Profiles of Brooks River pottery showing shapes: a, Smelt Creek; b, Brooks River Weir and Falls phases; c, Brooks River Camp phase; d, Pavik phase.

Figure 29 – Stone artifacts of the Brooks River Camp phase. Center, two characteristic lance blades of polished slate; top right and left, three blades of polished slate intended for insertion in a projectile head of antler or bone; bottom, wide lip ornament of jet to be inserted in a slot centered below the mouth. Scale is 6 inches (15 cm).

sunken tunnel from which people climbed upward into the house helped to preserve the heat.

All of these new Camp phase characteristics can be concluded to be northern in impetus, arriving in the Naknek region not later than AD 1100, according to available radiocarbon determinations, but very possibly a century earlier. Sites of this time have been explored most fully at Brooks River, but clear evidence of a Camp phase house has been recovered near the mouth of Smelt Creek on the middle Naknek River, and characteristic Camp phase artifacts radiocarbon-dated at about AD 1300 have been recovered at the very mouth of the river.

Unlike the sites of earlier times, those of the Camp phase at Brooks River were situated on sandy grounds that drained well, so that both artifacts of organic materials and remains of food animals were to some extent preserved in them. The artifacts included barbed antler or bone heads for harpoon darts that could be thrown with an atlatl in seal hunting on the coast, or used at closer quarters for fish in the interior; a dart head or very heavy arrow head, slotted to receive a slate tip; barbed bone arrowheads; wedges; awls; and a shaped but broken slab of whale bone that might have been part of a club. Preserved food trash made it clear that among land animals caribou provided a major resource, followed in order of quantity by beaver and porcupine. Remains of several wolves and one other canid, possibly a dog, were recovered.

excavated along Brooks River, were square in plan, of a single room, but departing from those of the earlier phases in being more deeply excavated into the contemporary ground surface, with heavy posts as supports of what was evidently a heavy, sod-covered roof. They departed especially in the tunnel entrance, now sunk at least a couple of feet more deeply into the ground than the floor of the house interior. While a central wood fire provided warmth in the main room, the

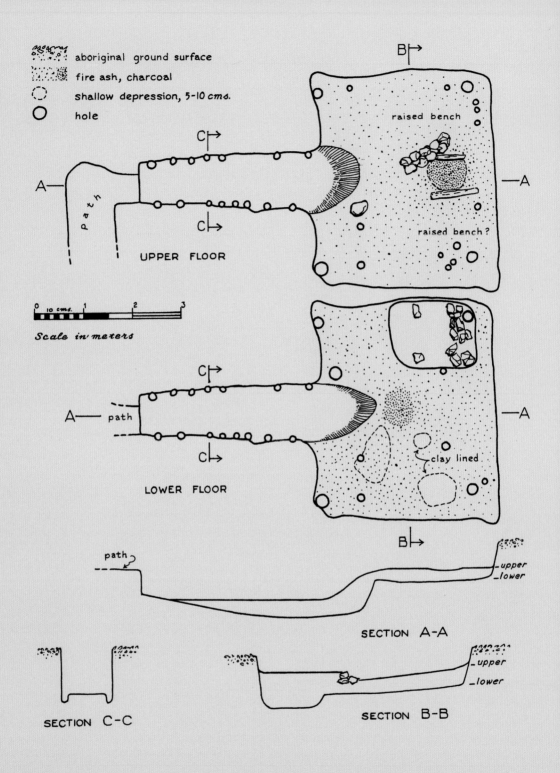

aboriginal ground surface

fire ash, charcoal

shallow depression, 5-10 cms.

hole

B →

C →

A —

Path

C →

UPPER FLOOR

raised bench

— A

raised bench?

0   10 cms.   1   2   3

Scale in meters

C →

A — path

C →

LOWER FLOOR

clay lined

— A

B →

path

_upper
_lower

SECTION A-A

SECTION C-C

SECTION B-B

_upper
_lower

Figure 30 – Plan and sections of a house of the Brooks River Camp phase, in which
the upper floor represented re-use of the house while preserving the same plan.
Charcoal from the lower floor was dated to about AD 1250.

In addition to the whale indicated by the bone fragment, sea mammals were represented by harbor seal; these must have been either traded to the interior or (more likely) harvested by the Brooks River people on seasonal visits to one or the other of the peninsula coasts. Fishes included — not surprisingly — salmon as the most plentiful, followed by char and other salmonids that are not further identifiable, but would have been either salmon or trout. Birds included remains of duck, goose, eagle, and gull. In short, subsistence was widely based on salmon and other fish, on caribou and seals, as well as on some smaller land animals and various birds.

Furthermore, in keeping with the increased maritime interest of Thule-tradition people in general, there was again an emphasis on the resources of the open coast of the Gulf of Alaska to the southwest. For by not long after AD 1100 a site on the Shelikof Strait coast evidenced what in archaeological terms can only be considered an occupation by people whose material possessions were in all details identical to those of the Camp phase of the Naknek region. It was apparently the result of the passage of Camp phase relatives across the mountains in sufficient number to establish a site that involved no significant amalgamation with local Pacific coastal people, but rather a settlement that was entirely an expression of the culture of the Bering Sea. [23]

The expansion of the Thule tradition

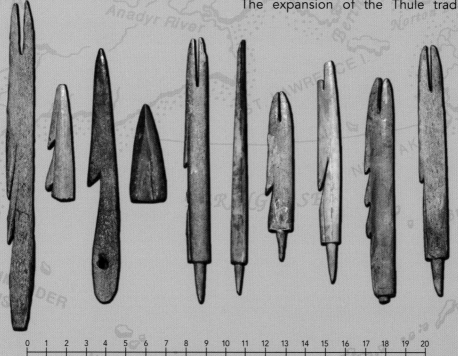

Figure 31 – Bone and antler artifacts of the Brooks River Camp phase. All are arrow or dart heads; those with the slotted tip were designed to accept a small slate blade, one of which is positioned fourth from the left. The third object from the left is the single certain example shown of a small harpoon head (possibly for fish), although the fragment immediately left of it may represent another. Scale is 20 cm.

throughout the arctic or winter-ice-fast coasts of America at the beginning of the second millennium AD has been shown by some investigators to be almost exactly parallel to the expansion of the Eskimoan language family, found in historic times from the tip of the Chukchi Peninsula of Asia to eastern Greenland, and from Point Barrow to Kodiak Island and Prince William Sound on the north Pacific. In general, estimates by linguists of the times at which the various Eskimoan languages have diverged from one another match the archaeological development of the Thule tradition — appearing first on the tip of the Asian mainland and at Bering Strait, then dividing into two prongs, one to northern Canada and Greenland, the other to southwestern Alaska. It is reasonable to think that the appearance of the Camp phase in the Naknek region reflects a portion of this linguistic and cultural expansion. Similarly, many diagnostic artifacts of that cultural movement, seen first on the Alaska Peninsula in the Brooks River Camp phase of AD 1100 or so, appeared a half-century or so later on the Kodiak group of islands, presumably reflecting a continuation of the same linguistic expansion. [24]

The parallel of language and tools would seem to mean that the sudden rise of the Camp phase of the Naknek region marks the arrival of a new people. At the same time, there is just enough continuity in certain respects between the Camp and preceding Falls phase to suggest that the Camp phase represents an amalgamation of (dominant) newcomers with older res-

idents. For example, at Brooks River the marked changes in pottery temper and form apparently occurred as a smooth but rapid transition, with the barrel-shaped pots of the Falls phase becoming more and more heavily tempered with pebbles before the shape actually changed to that of the Camp phase. A very few of the slate arrow or harpoon tips characteristic of the Camp phase have been recovered from otherwise Falls phase deposits at Brooks River, and although one can never be absolutely certain that they were not Camp phase possessions that were somehow out of place, they can also be interpreted as a more gradual manner of transition from one phase to the other without a complete break. Although Camp phase people all but gave up chipping for the finishing stage of stone implements, before their slate tools were polished they did shape them by chipping — rather than by sawing them to form with sharp whetstones, as was done at some other times and places in Alaska. All in all, it seems more likely that the Camp phase represents not a complete replacement of the earlier population by newcomers, but rather one in which newcomers, bringing a changed form of language and material culture, incorporated the former people. The comparable situation is even more pronounced on the Kodiak Archipelago, where many introductions of artifacts after about AD 1200 were clearly incorporated into the existing culture with relatively

little disruption. And yet the language must have changed toward the Alutiiq form of the Eskimoan speech current among the Kodiak people when they were met by arriving Russian fur hunters in the eighteenth century. [25]

The end of the Brooks River Camp phase in the Naknek region can be dated at about AD 1300 on the basis of radiocarbon determinations both from Camp phase residue and on remains of the succeeding Brooks River Bluffs phase. The people may not have gone willingly, however. As might well have been the case with the Brooks River Gravels phase of the Gomer period more than 2,000 years earlier, the Camp phase occupation seems to have terminated at the time of the deposit of a major layer of volcanic ash — ash C in Figure 6 — which like ash F has been suggested to represent an eruption that blanketed much of the Alaska Peninsula, this one, again, possibly centered at Aniakchak Volcano near Port Heiden far to the southwest. [26]

Brooks River Bluffs Phase –

How long it may have been after this eruption before the Naknek region was again occupied — this time by people of the Brooks River Bluffs phase — is not clear, although the radiocarbon evidence suggests that these successors appeared there not long after AD 1350. [27]

As the archaeology of the Naknek region was first explored, the appearance of continuity in terms of basic artifact categories led to the idea that the three phases of the Naknek period were linked in a relatively unbroken evolutionary progression, as had been the case with the phases of the Brooks River period. Causes of this appearance were the continuous use of polished slate implements, including fairly comparable forms of adze blades and knives; the continued emphasis on slate insert tips for arrowheads and harpoon heads; the manufacture of pottery in which small pebbles continued as the main tempering agent, despite considerable change in vessel form; and the (mistaken) assessment that the houses were similar — semisubterranean, with a single room entered by means of a more deeply sunken tunnel.

The first blow against this particular notion of continuity came with the suggestion by volcanologists that the heavy layer of volcanic ash C, consistently appearing between Camp phase and Bluffs-phase deposits at Brooks River, was the result of a massive eruptive event that may have blanketed most of the Alaska Peninsula, which would tend to suggest that the earlier Camp-phase people vacated the Naknek region in the aftermath of the explosion. The next blow involved a change in the perception of the nature of the houses of the Brooks River Bluffs phase and a concurrent recognition that the material culture of its people was virtually identical to that of contemporary Kodiak Island, while departing in significant ways from the Brooks River Camp phase that the Bluffs phase replaced. An increased sample of Bluffs-phase artifacts, developed both in National Park Service work at Brooks River in the 1980s and boosted by University of Oregon excavations on the lower Naknek River in the late 1990s, also made it more and more clear that despite the evident closeness in time of the Camp- and Bluffs-phase occupations, the collections of the two phases were clearly differentiated from one another in stylistically very recognizable ways, as though the replacement of the one by the other had actually involved two different peoples. [28]

In terms of portable artifacts, the distinction just mentioned between Bluffs and Camp phases is in most cases on the level of style rather than of more abstract categories. For instance, although slate insert tips for arrows and harpoons were among the most plentiful implements in both cases, the form of those of the Bluffs phase differed from a large proportion of those of the Camp phase. Polished stone adze blades were in both, but the zones in which the polish was applied tended to vary between the phases. With ulus, Bluff phase artifacts might be similar to those of the earlier phase, but some of them departed in having holes bored for attachment of the wooden handle. Large double-edged knives or lance blades were distinct in shape, those of Camp-phase form with the pronounced longitudinal ridges no longer appearing at all. Pebble-tempered pottery continued, although in some Bluffs phase sites it was less plentiful overall than it had been in those of the Camp phase, and the form was entirely different, with broader, flat bottoms and more erect sides that were also generally thinner, and often with horizontal ridges of clay running around the pot below the lip. The saucer-shaped clay lamp of the Camp phase, an

Figure 32 – Stone artifacts of the Brooks River Bluffs phase from the Leader Creek site, all of polished or partially polished stone. The objects at the lower left and upper right are ulu blades. The three in the upper center are projectile insert blades, the two below them are double-edged knives or lance heads. The object at upper left is an adze blade, lower right is a slate rod of unknown function, possibly a drill. Scale is 20 cm.

THE MORE ANCIENT PAST – Expansion in the Lower Drainage: The Naknek Period

Figure 33 – Designs engraved on incised pebbles of the Brooks River Bluffs phase, recovered in the course of excavations by the National Park Service in 2002-2003. Illustration by Barbara Bundy.

0   1   2 cm

implement that continued in common use around the Bering Sea coast to the north, vanished in the Naknek region and was replaced entirely by vessels of stone. In addition, entirely new Bluffs phase items included flat pebbles with light engraved designs, often of human-like forms, that were essentially identical to engravings on slate pebbles known in the late prehistoric period in the Kodiak Archipelago as well as farther south along the Gulf of Alaska coast. Finally, upon reinterpretation it was especially clear that the most common houses of the Brooks River Bluffs phase were distinctly different from those of the earlier phase, and that they were similar in basic form to contemporary houses on Kodiak Island.

When houses of what came to be recognized as the Bluffs phase were first examined and briefly tested during the Katmai Project of the 1950s, the complexes of apparently interconnected surface depressions were interpreted as semisubterranean houses of multiple rooms. Although it was a Bluffs-phase house that we found in 1960 with our own first excavations on the bank of Brooks River, we exposed only a part of a single room with its sunken tunnel entrance, and we interpreted it as a house of one room. In hindsight, it was almost certainly part of a multiroom structure that had otherwise been eroded away by the stream. Nevertheless, when we attempted to clear what looked on the surface to be another late prehistoric house, this one of several rooms, we found that the depressions with Bluffs phase floors were located in the top of a much older midden in which there were traces of many separate occupations dating to various times over more than 3,000 years. Ancient digging had left the area so confused that we were unable to trace the form of the supposed multiroom house in any convincing way. And when we found that two of the Bluffs phase "rooms" were equipped with sunken entrance tunnels, we concluded that the tunnels must be entrances from the outside into separate houses, and that the only reason the visible complex of surface depressions had given the impression of a multiroom structure was the very complexity of the digging for various houses that had occurred through history. We decided that Bluffs phase houses, like the other ancient habitations that were becoming known along Brooks River, were confined to structures of one room. So fixed was this idea that when National Park Service excavations of the 1980s (led by one of my former students) revealed a large semisubterranean Bluffs-phase structure with side rooms radiating from it, the side rooms were interpreted as different houses on which the central "house" had been superimposed at a later date.

A reinterpretation was finally driven by results of research on the Kodiak group of islands that showed that multiroom houses there characterized settlements of both the late prehistoric and early historic periods. [29] Finally, then, almost all of the Bluffs-phase houses were recognized as having been in plan quite different from those of the Camp phase. Although a central room with its fireplace was entered from outside by a deeply sunken tunnel, subsidiary rooms radiated from the main room like spokes of a wheel, many of them connected to it by means of a sunken entryway. Contents of these rooms indicated they had served different purposes and the

overall house size suggested a larger and more extended family in residence. The form of the house, then, like the small engravings and the lamps of stone, harks to contemporaneous features found on the Kodiak group of islands.

The conclusion from all of this, simply, is that the reoccupation of the Naknek region following the volcanic eruption of about AD 1300 was by a people directly affiliated with those of Kodiak Island, whether they originated precisely on that island or from somewhere nearby. This is underlined by the fact that people of the northern Alaska Peninsula who are the recent descendants of those of the Bluffs phase spoke a language classed by linguists as a form of Alutiiq, the Native speech of Kodiak and the northern coast of the Gulf of Alaska. [30]

Even more obviously than those of the Camp phase, the people of this Bluffs phase were settled over much of the extent of the Naknek River drainage. Their living sites were first excavated near upper Naknek Lake at Brooks River, as minor explorations indicated similar and contemporary sites along the Savonoski River still higher in the drainage system. Later, further testing along the course of the Naknek River itself led to the recognition of a major site near the mouth of Big Creek and another near the mouth of Leader Creek; more scattered artifacts appeared downstream from Leader Creek, but within the area heavily developed by canneries and related enterprises that have masked the presence of earlier

Bluffs-phase houses. It became clear that there were definite settlements on both the upper and lower Naknek River as well as on streams tributary to the upper portions of Naknek Lake. Whether this represents a more complete coverage of the drainage system by this people than had been the case in any earlier phase is not absolutely certain, what with limits to explorations in some areas and the extent of tidal erosion on the lower Naknek River. But it is certainly evident that the Bluffs phase people were interested in the entire drainage area. That much recognized, the reevaluation of Bluffs phase house form was validated by excavations at the Leader Creek site in 1998-99, by excavations by archaeologists of the Bureau of Indian Affairs at the site near the mouth of Big Creek, and by still later explorations by the National Park Service in a major Bluffs-phase site at Brooks River. [31]

Like the Camp-phase deposits, those of the Bluffs phase preserved some limited amounts of organic material. Artifacts included barbed bone arrowheads, whale bone slabs, and wedges of bone and antler. Faunal remains included especially caribou, but also beaver, porcupine, bear, wolf, hare, marmot, and otter among land animals; harbor seal and a few spotted seal among sea

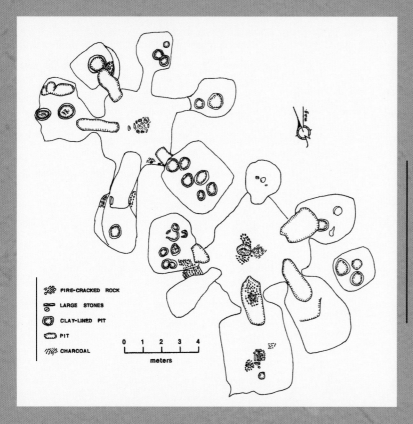

FIRE-CRACKED ROCK
LARGE STONES
CLAY-LINED PIT
PIT
CHARCOAL

0 1 2 3 4
meters

Figure 34 – Plan drawing of a pair of houses of the Brooks River Bluffs phase, from the site at Leader Creek. The bluff along the Naknek River is a short distance to the south.

mammals; duck, goose, loon, cormorant, eagle, gull, and ptarmigan among birds; and red, silver, and king salmon among fishes. In addition, the site at Leader Creek, closest to the river mouth, included partial remains of several beluga. Again, a wide range in subsistence is indicated, with the taking of beluga especially significant, since the live weight of those animals is so much greater than that of any of the other mammals represented. The special staples at Leader Creek in terms of quantity of food were beluga, caribou, and of course salmon.

Clearly, the Bluffs-phase inhabitants were successful at living off the Naknek regional landscape. What, then, brought the phase to an end? In this case, we are fortunate to have some recorded historical details.

Pavik Phase:
Invasion and Displacement [32] –
Archaeologically, the most dramatically recognizable element of partial disruption in the continuity of the Naknek period came with the sudden appearance of European objects at the Paugvik site in the Pavik phase: glass trade beads; metal projectile insert tips as well as slate ones; steel axe heads replacing stone adze blades; some metal knives joining the older slate knives; a few fragments of chinaware alongside the still plentiful aboriginal pottery.[33] Nevertheless, Pavik-phase articles that were still of obviously local manufacture were not substantially unlike those of their immediate predecessors, which seemed to argue for a continuity of Native occupants.

Full awareness that such a diagnosis of continuity was a rash misunderstanding came from certain historical accounts. These indicated that the people met at the mouth of the Naknek River by arriving Russians were, like those of other communities around Bristol Bay, actually recently arrived immigrants from the Kuskokwim River region who had displaced earlier inhabitants to the interior at some time around AD 1800.

The Russian discovery of the Aleutian Islands and portions of the southern Alaska mainland was by the expedition under Vitus Bering that sailed from Kamchatka in 1741. Within ten years Russian fur-hunting voyages to the Aleutian Islands were common, and by 1759 the hunters had reached the easternmost part of the island chain. In 1784 Russian fur hunters under Shelikov established the first lasting settlement on Kodiak Island and by this time or shortly after there was also a small Russian fur-hunting station at the Native settlement of Katmai, located in Katmai Bay on the Shelikof Strait coast of the Alaska Peninsula. [34]

The Native people the Russians met here they called "Aleuts." They had applied this term to the Unangan people of the Aleutian Archipelago, and then extended it to the people of the Kodiak region (now customarily known as Koniag, or especially *Alutiit*, singular *Alutiiq*) despite the fact that they recognized that the people so described spoke a language distinct from that of people of the Aleutians. As will be seen, however, when they encountered the various peoples living on the coasts of Bristol Bay and along the rivers and lakes farther north and east, they began to recognize separate ethnic groups such as "Aglegmiut" (now *Aglurmiut*) around the head of Bristol Bay, Kiatiirmiut of the upper Nushagak River region and around Iliamna Lake, and Kusquqvagmiut, from the Kuskokwim River, from around Togiak, and from the upper Nushagak region. These people were distinguished by those terms from the "Aleuts" of the interior and southeastern coast of the Alaska Peninsula, and of Kodiak. Furthermore, they are now recognized as speakers not of Alutiiq but of Central Yupik. [35]

In the late 1770s, a Russian hunting detachment serving under Potap K. Zaikov had camped for several years on the False Pass side of Unimak Island and presumably explored portions of the Bristol Bay coast of the Alaska Peninsula. But just when outsiders first made contact with Native people specifically of the Naknek region is not entirely clear, although the year 1791 may hold that honor. That appears to have been when an actual visit to the mouth of the Naknek River and to Paugvik was made by a hunting party under Vasilii Medvednikov and Dmitri Bocharov, the latter of whom recorded his Alaska Peninsula explorations of that year in a map marking portage routes across the peninsula — one of them by way of what is now Becharof Lake, a body of water named for him with a slight change in spelling. Not included, however, was any

indication of a route across Katmai Pass and by way of Naknek Lake and River, an area left blank on Bocharov's map. [36]

It is presumably as a result of such contacts as these that when Petr Korsakovskii visited Paugvik in 1818 — after crossing from Kodiak to the Bristol Bay coast by way of Katmai, Puale Bay, Lake Becharof and the Egegik River — he found that the Paugvik people were already accustomed to trade with Russian fur hunters. This despite the fact that the trading post on the lower Nushagak River, Aleksandrovsk Redoubt, was not established until the following year. [37] Earlier trade could have involved the station at Katmai — although if so, there is no indication that any Katmai trade proceeded along a route by way of the Severnovsk settlements of the region immediately upstream of Naknek Lake. Indeed, there is a hint in Korsakovskii's journal of 1818 that at least some of the Severnovsk people were unfriendly both to inhabitants of Katmai and to the Russians. For although at least two Severnovsk *toyons* (important men) were among the guides of Korsakovskii's party, when the group reached Katmai they were told that other Severnovsk men were lurking nearby intent on murder. The party passed this potential hazard without harm, however, and in due time arrived at Paugvik.

In Korsakovskii's journal Paugvik was described as occupied by "Aglegmiut" (i.e., Aglurmiut), who were said to have been driven from their former territory (location undisclosed) to arrive at the mouth of the Naknek River. The Russian party was regaled at Paugvik with a dance, at which at least 400 Native people were said to be present. [38]

More complete and slightly later Russian sources added more information: The Aglurmiut had been driven from the lower Kuskokwim River region by warfare, and on their arrival at the head of Bristol Bay they forced out the inhabitants of peninsular coastal settlements to interior Severnovsk

apparently able to bring to a halt, and they found the Aglurmiut thereafter to be their useful employees and allies. [39]

That is, whatever the conclusions to be drawn from the archaeological collection of tools, the historical information makes it clear that the Aglurmiut of the settlement of Paugvik were newcomers who had arrived at the mouth of the Naknek River sometime around AD 1800, and that they were a group distinct from those inhabitants of the

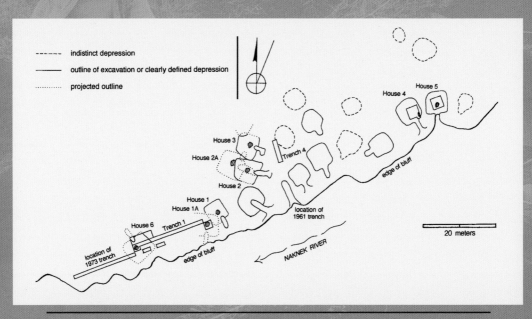

Figure 35 – Plan of the Paugvik site when it was excavated between 1961 and 1985. Three house floors were cleared completely (those numbered 1 - 3), with three others subjected to more limited tests (4 - 6).

(Savonoski as Americans would later call it), and to Ugashik. When the Russian post of Alexandrovsk Redoubt was established at Nushagak in 1819, the Aglurmiut, established at the mouths of the rivers Nushagak, Kvichak, Naknek, and Egegik, were warring with their immediate neighbors up the streams. This fighting the Russians were

Naknek drainage who were grouped around Severnovsk. This distinction is strongly reinforced by information from Russian Orthodox Church records that will be drawn on in a chapter to follow.

As a people originating in the more northerly regions, it is not surprising that some of the Aglurmiut characteristics hint at a return to certain practices of the earlier phase of northerners, the Brooks River Camp phase. In the Pavik phase these returns to the past included the family use of semisubterranean houses of a single room with central fireplace and deeply sunken entrance tunnel, and the reappearance of the saucer-shaped clay lamp for burning sea mammal oil. Although it was almost certainly present earlier, the site at Paugvik has been concluded to have included a men's house or *kashim* located among the single-room family houses. Beyond these, portable artifacts of local manufacture in stone included especially slate projectile insert tips for both harpoons and arrows, a few knives of polished slate, and a very few adze blades. As noted earlier, however, the majority of cutting implements were of metal; these included ulu and knife blades, axes, and some wedges. Also recovered were parts of some metal pots, which were augmented by a very few chinaware vessels.

Because in the dense peaty ground at the Paugvik site a portion of the deposit remained frozen throughout summers, the preservation of organic material was enormously better than in any of the earlier sites we had worked in. Thus the site provided a richer inventory of bone, antler, and a few ivory objects, as well as numerous items of wood, all of which gave a much better picture of the daily life of the people than was obtained from earlier phases. These finds included a few harpoon heads of antler and ivory, as well as harpoon foreshafts and socket pieces, some dart heads, bone arrow-heads, wooden bow fragments, sled parts, kayak pieces, parts of fish lures, pieces of compound vessels of wood and birch bark, spoons and spatulas of antler, bone heads for picks and shovels, rake heads of antler, and small wooden carvings that at one time must have adorned masks. Wooden skin stretchers gave proof of local efforts in the Russian-encouraged trapping for furs. There were also segments of grass matting, and a few pieces of leather. As indicated earlier, pottery was chiefly tempered with small pebbles of water-worn gravel, now shaped with relatively erect walls and flat bases — in fact, more similar to pottery of the immediately preceding Brooks River Bluffs phase than to the earlier (northern?) pottery of the Camp phase. An exception to the pebble tempering was the case of the saucer-shaped clay lamps, which were tempered with grass, and fired only slightly or not at all.

The only really plentiful imported objects were glass beads in several patterns, most of which must have once adorned clothing. Actually, in view of evidence of participation in the fur trade under Russian management, the sum total of European objects was surprisingly small, strong evidence that the Russian traders were stingy with their goods. Some of these, of course, like the tobacco and tea soon in general use, were not the kind to leave traces among the material objects recovered when we dug at Paugvik. [40]

THE MORE ANCIENT PAST – Expansion in the Lower Drainage: The Naknek Period

The Paugvik site, from which several local people have made collections of artifacts eroding from the river bluff, was first sampled briefly by archaeologists in 1948. [41] In 1961 and 1973 it was trenched and partly mapped by our parties from the University

throughout the nineteenth century and into the period following the American purchase of Alaska in 1867. Instead, we found that there were no trade materials in the site that would show it was occupied into the period after which

Figure 36 – Excavations in progress at the Paugvik site, 1985.

of Oregon, and in 1985 we addressed it again and more comprehensively with a larger crew from the University of Oregon and the Field Museum of Natural History in Chicago, [42] when several houses were excavated. The dating we arrived at on the basis of historical evidence and of artifacts of the collection itself, was something of a surprise to us. From historical accounts already mentioned and to be described more fully later, we were already reasonably certain that the settlement at the point we excavated had been in use by 1818. We had presumed the site would also provide indications of occupation

commercial salteries or canneries for the U.S. market were in the area, or even into the American period at all. An ending date not later than about AD 1870 was reasonable. Yet it appears that the name "Paugvik" continued in use somewhat longer, apparently designating an area upstream from our excavations and within the modern village of Naknek, as will be mentioned later. In any event, the area of Paugvik covered by the excavations carried out in all of the years indicated can be dated only from somewhere around AD 1800 to possibly 1870 — by which time written history takes over, as we shall see.

Figure 37 – Artifacts of the Pavik phase. Left, ulu with a slate blade and wooden handle; right, iron transverse knife above a bone arrow or dart head, and a (rare) stone adze blade. Center, a blade of brass to be inserted in a projectile head, above five assorted glass beads. The scale is 20 cm.

Unexplored Sites of the Upper Drainage –

And now, what of the people who were displaced inland by the Aglurmiut at the beginning of the nineteenth century? These were presumably descendants of those folk of the Brooks River Bluffs phase who had been spread throughout the Naknek drainage region. Further, as will be emphasized in the next chapter, these displaced people can with confidence be recognized as speakers of the language now most commonly referred to as Alutiiq, in contrast to the Central Yupik spoken by the Aglurmiut. In the nineteenth century historical sources there are references to sites of these Severnovsk people, as they were called, in two places. One of these was near the mouth of the westward flowing Savonoski River, a point which coincides with the terminus of the northward flowing Ukak River as the two streams empty almost together at the extreme eastern end of Iliuk Arm of Naknek Lake. The other location was apparently near the outlet of the short Grosvenor River, which drains Grosvenor Lake and joins the Savonoski at a point about ten miles or so above its mouth.

Although there have been examinations of these areas by archaeologists, visits have been brief and no definitive collections have been made. Indeed, sites have been recorded in both of those areas, and along the lowermost Savonoski River the site area is more than a half-mile in length, with house depressions strung out along a set of former dunes — at the eastern end of which are the remains of the village forcibly abandoned in 1912 with the volcanic eruption. But there is no archaeological confirmation of the presence of settlements in either area that date specifically from the period of Russian control, although Russian historical documents are clear enough that such settlements did exist.

Furthermore, there is no known evidence of any Russian-period settlement at Brooks River, which is the most closely explored area of the entire drainage system; and somewhat less intensive surveys of the Naknek River have produced no absolute evidence of any settlement of that period upstream of Paugvik, although there is one possible small site above the rapids on the upper course of the Naknek River. In other words, both archaeological and historical evidence seem to say that during the Russian period there was an unoccupied zone from the very head of Naknek Lake to at least the Naknek rapids, and possibly to the mouth of the Naknek River — a no-man's-land of at least 45 and perhaps more than 65 miles as a boat paddles.

Given this circumstance, one expects that people newly confined to the upper drainage would vary somewhat in their material culture from the Aglurmiut newcomers of the Pavik phase. Indeed, a label has been suggested for just such a projected archaeological phase,[43] but it is premature: for by definition an archaeological phase of culture is based on a set of objects, a collection, that can be considered representative of the material culture of a specific group of people. With no collection yet made from the interior that is contemporary with the Pavik phase of Paugvik, there is nothing on which to base a definition.

In 1953, when the Severnovsk area in the general vicinity of the settlement abandoned in 1912 was first examined by archaeologists, three rather modest test cuts were made. These were in or near complexes of depressions the excavators thought from surface indications to represent former multiroom houses. The very few objects recovered are indeed comparable to artifacts of the Brooks River Bluffs phase — some slate ulu fragments, fragmentary projectile insert blades of slate, a bone harpoon head with a line hole, a small stone lamp — but they were undated except to recognize that they were below the volcanic ash of the 1912 eruption; no metal or glass or other such imported objects were found. In the early 1960s, others of us dug small test pits in the same area, confirming the stratigraphic relationship — including the recognition that the occupation was below what we had termed volcanic ash B as well as the ash A of the 1912 event — but we recovered no artifacts. In 2001, a National Park Service party spent three days at the site, mapped it, and excavated a single small test in the

THE MORE ANCIENT PAST – Expansion in the Lower Drainage: The Naknek Period

presumed central room of a multiroom house located at the extreme west end of the known site area, closest to the present mouth of the Ukak River. They found no artifacts, but they obtained a radiocarbon measurement on charcoal thought to be from the floor. The result of this, the only radiocarbon age to be derived so far from that site near the mouth of the Savonoski River, is 100 ± 60 years.

If this age could seriously be taken as that of one or more of the multiroom structures tentatively identified along the lower Savonoski River, it might certainly indicate a continuation there of the modes of houses, at least, of the earlier Brooks River Bluffs phase, and would allow one to suspect that the Bluffs phase itself had endured in the inland regions into and perhaps even beyond the nineteenth century, hence being contemporaneous with the Pavik phase downstream. Unfortunately, however, radiocarbon ages of anything less than 250 years are notoriously unreliable; this recent period is that in which, first, the industrial uses of coal and oil as fuels have filled the upper atmosphere with particles of ancient

Figure 38 – Entrances to sod-covered houses in the Severnovsk village of Nunamiut on the bank above the Savonoski River. Photo by J.D. Sayres, 1918, National Geographic Society Katmai Expeditions, courtesy Archives and Manuscripts Department, University of Alaska Anchorage.

carbon, and, second, atomic testing has blasted radioactive materials into the same atmosphere. Both of these circumstances have had unmeasurable skewing effects on the ages of carbon particles in the atmosphere that are incorporated into living plants and animals and which finally become involved in the dating process.

The 1953 research also produced a description and partial plan of dwellings that were evidently in use at the time the early twentieth-century settlement was abandoned. These consisted of a single rectangular room about 10 x 12 feet in size, with walls of upright split cottonwood logs. They were entered by a short entryway about 4 feet long and 2 1/2 feet wide that was intruded into one of the narrow sides that looked toward the river; there was a window set into the rear wall opposite the entrance. With the exception evidently of the window and the entry door, the entire structure with its nearly flat, split log roof, was banked over with sod. Although the drawings make it appear that the houses had been dug somewhat into the ground, so much dirt, pumice, and other debris had slumped into them by 1953 that no relevant measurement was obtained.[44] When this single-room house plan came into use, which contrasts so markedly with the evidence of earlier multi-room houses in the same area, is unknown.

In short, although it is reasonable to expect that there is a contrast to be recognized between the material objects in use by people of the Pavik phase and those in use by contemporary upriver people of the Severnovsk area, the information that would permit it has not yet been collected. The local record is incomplete.

Notes

[1] Very recently, a site dated about 27,000 radiocarbon years ago has been reported within 50 miles of the arctic coast of Siberia at a point west of Chukotka province and about a thousand miles west of the Bering Strait (Pitulko et al. 2004). Whether it may relate to early migrants to the New World is thus far unknown. Otherwise, as one approaches the Bering Strait region the only substantial collection of early tools of any kind with associated early radiocarbon dates is actually from the Kamchatka Peninsula, rather than Chukotka, where most materials are undated. The Kamchatkan sites at Ushki Lake have been reported to produce radiocarbon ages of about 14,000 years (e.g., Dikov and Titov 1984), but recent redating suggests an age closer to 11,000 radiocarbon years (Goebel et al. 2003) — a date later than some of those obtained from sites in Alaska.

[2] For an animated flooding of the land bridge, go to http://www.ncdc.noaa.gov/paleo/parcs/atlas/beringia/lbridge.html

[3] We here sidestep discussion of an apparent paradox that bedevils American archaeologists. That Native peoples of both North and South America are strongly Northeast Asian in genetic makeup, is widely agreed, with the reasonable supposition that their earliest ancestors entered the Americas through what is now Alaska. But whereas the earliest sites in North America are conservatively dated to around 12,000 BC or even slightly later, others in South America are reputedly as old, with one accepted by many archaeologist to be dated at least as early as 12,500 BC. Furthermore, these artifact collections, many of which include varieties of impressive chipped stone spear or lance points, bear little resemblance to the earliest (microblade-bearing) remains from Alaska. Thus, if the ancestors of these ancient southern people were able to sneak past the glaciers of the late Pleistocene in Alaska, they left no presently recognized traces there. To make matters worse, in the last few decades, many geologists have concluded that there was no pathway through the glaciers for most, and perhaps all, of this late glacial period. Ironically, then, as grassland conditions on Beringia appear to have been the most favorable for enticing humans to move from Asia to America without a major change in their basic mode of living, there appears to have been no accessible interior path into heartland America.

[4] It has recently been reported by R. Guthrie (2004) that mammoths survived to around 8000 radiocarbon years ago, and as late as 5, 700 years ago by D. Veltre et al. (personal communication) on St. Paul Island in the Pribilof Islands, Bering Sea.

[5] A summary of the major views on these subjects, many of which are not relevant here, can be found in a single issue of the journal Arctic Anthropology which presents results of a symposium assembled by Bever and Kunz (2001). Although there is no intellectual problem in deriving the microblade makers ultimately from Siberia sometime in the Pleistocene, the particular line of descent of the other, plains-like people is at this point not yet the subject of agreement among archaeologists.

[6] The source for this is Henn (1978). This Ugashik Narrows phase has been considered a part of what has been designated the American Paleoarctic tradition, which in Alaska lasts overall from about 12,000 to 7000 radiocarbon years ago.

[7] The source for this description, as for the majority of those from the immediate Naknek and Naknek River region, is Dumond (1981).

[8] The references for Ugashik Narrows and Graveyard Point are those cited above in earlier notes.

[9] This period was named more than twenty years ago (Dumond 1981), based on the sound of a word said to have once designated the Brooks River region. Since then, this earlier name for the river has appeared in print as Kidawik Creek in a quotation from 1920 (Clemens and Norris 1999:159). Had I known of this earlier spelling, Kidawik would have been the name of the period.

[10] This designation was introduced in Dumond (1977).

[11]Dumond (1981:128).

[12] The Kobuk River site is described by Anderson (1988). The Ugashik structure is in Henn (1978), that on the Kvichak reported by Holmes and McMahan (1996).

[13] Described by Workman and Zollars (2002).

[14] A more complete description of these sites in Siberia and Canada is in Dumond (1977). The earliest Seward Peninsula dates are reported by Harritt (1994:216-217).

[15] Attempts to adduce continuity of occupation after the Arctic Small Tool period on the Chukchi Sea coast include arguments by Giddings and Anderson (1986:314), questioned by Dumond (2000). The possibility of Aniakchak-area volcanic debris at Brooks River is referred to by Riehle et al. (2000). Evidence for major fluctuations in the magnitude of fish runs in the region during the past two millennia is provided by Finney et al. (2002).

[16] Exploration of Norton cultural remains on Norton Bay is described by Giddings (1964); related material at Point Hope, described there as "Near Ipiutak," is treated by Larsen and Rainey (1948); that near the northeastern corner of Alaska is reported by MacNeish (1956). That the various Norton-related cultures could be conceptualized as a tradition was first detailed by Dumond (1977). A set of varied papers discussing Norton remains is to be found in Shaw and Holmes (1982), and a more recent discussion is by Dumond (2000).

[17] This is suggested in Riehle et al. (2000).

[18] The inclusion in pottery clay of non-plastic elements such as fiber (hair, fine tree roots, etc.), sand and fine gravel, or ground stone or pulverized potsherds, is in order to control shrinkage and lessen cracking while the pot is dried thoroughly before firing — a step necessary to prevent the pot from exploding because of steam generated by any remaining internal moisture.

[19] The general description is in Dumond (1981). Information regarding further testing includes National Park Service clearance forms plus a pair of unpublished reports, Smith (1990) and Bland et al. (1998), both of which in my opinion treat primarily Weir phase remains.

[20] Sites of the Bering Sea include some from outer Bristol Bay not yet reported in the literature, and others from Nunivak Island (Nowak 1982), whereas evident whaling harpoon heads are reported from the Norton-related Near Ipiutak culture of Point Hope on the Chukchi Sea (Larsen and Rainey 1948).

[21] The sites on the Shelikof Strait coast closest to the Naknek region, involving the Takli Cottonwood and Kukak Beach phases, are described by G. H. Clark (1977), those at the mouth of the Ugashik River by Henn (1978).

[22] This usage was first set out in Dumond (1977). It is essentially the same as what some other researchers have termed the Northern Maritime tradition (e.g., Collins 1964).

[23] This involves the Kukak Mound phase described by G. H. Clark (1977).

[24]This as a part of the Eskimoan linguistic expansion has been treated by Dumond (e.g., 1988, 2003). Linguists providing related information include Leer (1991) and Woodbury (1984). The distribution of the Eskimoan languages is mapped by Krauss (1982).

[25] In fairness to archaeologists working on Kodiak, it must be said that many, probably most of them, are unwilling to conceive of the introduction of new speech to the archipelago in the early second millennium AD. This is at odds with the opinion of some key linguists, who have suggested that ancestral Alutiiq has been present on Kodiak only for a thousand years or less (Leer 1991). The situation is, however, aside from the point of the present summary.

[26] Suggested, again, by Riehle et al. (2000).

[27] Earlier descriptions of the Bluffs phase are in Dumond (1981) and Harritt (1988), a modified view in Dumond (2003).

[28] The possible significance of volcanic ash C is remarked in Riehle et al. (2000). Further details

regarding the contrast between the Camp and Bluffs phases is in Dumond (2003).

[29] The notion of houses held in 1953 is indicated by Davis (1954). The form of relevant houses on Kodiak is described by Knecht and Jordan (1985) and Knecht (1995). The change in understanding of the Bluffs-phase house form is explained by Dumond (1994, 2003).

[30] See again Leer (1991), who finds that differences among Alutiiq dialects suggest that their divergence occurred within no more than the last several hundred years.

[31] The site at Leader Creek is described by Dumond (2003); the site at Big Creek is reported by O'Leary (1998); recent work at Brooks River is reported by Bundy et al. (2005).

[32] The designation for this archaeological phase was taken from the report of a visit to the Naknek region in 1948 by archaeologists who reported "Pavik" to have been the name of the earlier Native community on the north bank of the Naknek River near its mouth (Larsen 1950), with its consequent use as a phase label appearing in print long ago (e.g., Dumond 1962). It is now certain that the spelling "Paugvik" more closely approximates local Native usage. "Pavik" is retained for the archaeological unit, however, simply to eliminate any chance of misunderstanding of earlier literature, whereas the settlement will be consistently referred to as Paugvik.

[33] This organization of results was presented in Dumond (1981); although the immigrant nature of the Pavik phase people was beginning to be understood at the time, it was not then seen as highly significant in terms of Native material culture..

[34] Solovjova and Vovnyanko (2002:App. IV, p. 308)) list the date of the founding of the Russian artel at Katmai as 1782, although without providing a specific reference. Discussions in their text indicate only that the Katmai post was functioning in the earliest years of the Three Saints settlement.

[35] Wrangell (1980:62 [translated from an earlier source]). Alutiiq is now considered the southernmost of the Yupik division of the Eskimoan languages and distinct from Central Yupik (e.g., Woodbury 1984).

[36] Solovjova and Vovnyanko (2002) refer both to the False Pass camp of the 1770s (p. 224) and to the 1791 contact with Paugvik (p. 156, and App. IV, p. 308), although the sources they draw on are not clearly indicated, and they also mention the Bocharov peninsular explorations and map (pp. 192-193).

[37] Fedorova (1973:136-139) discusses the correct date for the establishment of the Aleksandrovsk establishment.

[38] VanStone (1988) provides a translation of Korsakovskii's journal of 1818. See also Dumond and VanStone (1995:6-7).

[39] Important additional details were provided in 1839 by Wrangell (translated as Wrangell 1980). Modern summaries of the Aglurmiut background are by Ackerman and Ackerman (1973) and Fienup-Riordan (1990), with the particular Paugvik history summarized in Dumond and VanStone (1995) and Dumond (2003).

[40] A complete report on the collection from Paugvik, constituting the Pavik archaeological phase, is in Dumond and VanStone (1995).

[41] Larsen (1950).

[42] Dumond (1981), Dumond and VanStone (1995).

[43] Harritt (1997).

[44] The work in 1953, including the description of the abandoned houses, is by Davis (1954), with a version of his drawing reproduced by Clemens and Norris (1999:21). Brief tests in the 1960s are mentioned in Dumond (1981:59), the work of 2001 in Hilton (2002), where the laboratory number of the radiocarbon determination is listed as Beta-159784; because of its short measured age, the date cannot be calibrated.

The Nineteenth Century

The Korsakovskii expeditions of 1818 and 1819 to Bristol Bay and beyond failed to result in a map of the Naknek region. Credit for the first that is known is owed to explorations by a party led by Ivan Ya. Vasil'ev ten years later, in 1829. Vasil'ev's map shows some features of his route across the northern Alaska Peninsula from Katmai to Paugvik, evidently by way of daunting Katmai Pass, unlike the crossing by that earlier expedition. Departing Katmai in March, the party reached Naknek Lake and followed it (on skis) to the outlet river and finally to Bristol Bay, apparently bypassing the Severnovsk settlements, possibly taking a route south of Mt. Katolinat and along present Margot Creek to the lake shore. Although Iliuk Arm seems to be referred to in Vasil'ev's journal (called "Napuan Illyuk Lake") as an appendage of Naknek Lake proper, there is no indication on his map of any settlement on the strangely shaped

Figure 40 – Composite rendition of the Vasil'ev maps. The two village labels at the mouth of the Naknek River are from his map of 1829; the overall form, the trails, and all other labels are those of the later map of 1831-32; spellings are transliterated directly from his Russian labels.

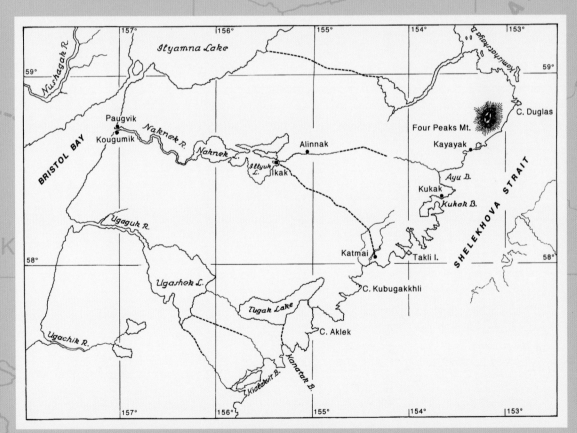

body of water. In contrast, Paugvik and a settlement labeled Kougumik are shown on the right and left banks of the Naknek River at its mouth. [1]

In the next couple of years Vasil'ev also explored portions of the Gulf of Alaska coast along the Alaska Peninsula. This work resulted in a somewhat modified map of the northern peninsula in which the shape of Naknek Lake was changed a bit, and two settlements were indicated between Naknek Lake and Shelikof Strait on a portage route that appears to follow the Savonoski River above Iliuk Arm, although the river itself is not specifically indicated. One of these, *Ikak*, is at the head of Iliuk Arm; the other, labeled *Alinnak*, is some distance to the east at what could easily be the point at which the Grosvenor Lake outlet river joins the Savonoski. [2]

This latter is the point where one, or possibly even two, sites tested archaeologically appeared to have been occupied until the time of the 1912 eruption. Interestingly enough, as mentioned in the preceding chapter, no sites of the nineteenth or early twentieth century have thus far been identified anywhere in the Naknek drainage area between the upper end of Iliuk Arm and the rapids area of the Naknek River, a linear distance of some 45 miles. This suggests that the warfare reported between the Aglurmiut and those earlier people of the Brooks River Bluffs archaeological phase had resulted not only in the displacement of the latter, but also in an unpopulated segment of the middle drainage. [3]

Ethnic Groups

Records with greater detail regarding the Native inhabitants of the region waited on the arrival in Russian America of Orthodox priests. Not the first, but certainly the most famous of these, Ivan Veniaminov arrived in Unalaska in 1823 to establish the church there; in records for the year 1827-28 there is a simple reference to "Severnovsk Aleuts" without additional detail. With Aleksandrovsk Redoubt as a part of his assigned territory, in 1829 and some later years Veniaminov visited that Nushagak post, promoting the baptism of Natives in the vicinity. It was apparently in large part from Veniaminov's influence — after his transfer to Sitka and appointment as the first Orthodox bishop in Russian America — that in 1842 a church mission was formally established at Nushagak, and thereafter the settlements at the mouth of the Naknek River were included within its territory.

The first actual reference to the Naknek region in church documents, however, relates to the previous year. For in 1841, the Kodiak church establishment recorded the baptism of 46 individuals (babies to elderly adults) in the Severnovsk settlements, evidently on the same missionizing trip in which 57 individuals were baptized at Katmai. In 1844, however, the settlements of Ugashik, Ikak, and "Alikak" (an error for Alinak or Alinnak?) were added to the territory managed by the priest of the Nushagak mission, and thereafter any mention of a priestly visit to the Naknek region involved one from

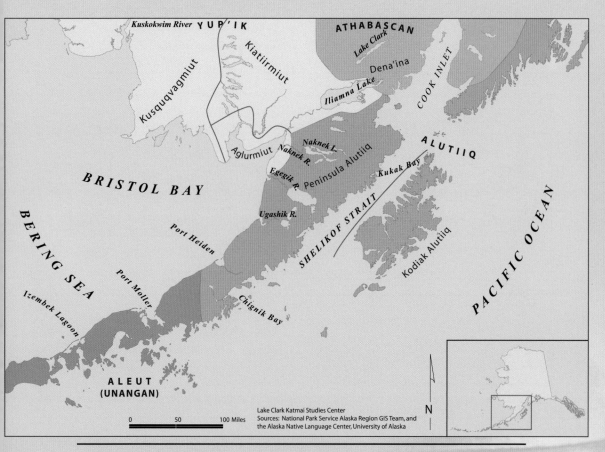

Figure 41 – Distribution of nineteenth-century Native ethnic groups and languages in the vicinity of the Alaska Peninsula (Dumond 2003, esp. Figs. 1.2, 1.4, with sources indicated; spellings of ethnic names follow current usage).

the Nushagak (Aleksandrovsk) station. [4]   The implication, then, is that in addition to ethnic groups known to the Russians as "Aglegmiut" (Aglurmiut), "Kiatintsy" (now *Kiatiirmiut*), and "Kuskokvimtsy" (now *Kusquqvagmiut*), the Nushagak Mission also took on regular religious ministration to Alutiiq people of the Alaska Peninsula, designated at the time as "Aleut." A few decades later in the century the Nushagak priest also was reporting official visits to Katmai with its "Aleuts," as well.

The continued recognition of distinctions in Native ethnic groups is indicated in Russian Church documents such as those synthesized in Table 1. Two somewhat different bits of information can be drawn from this.

The first of these bits is simply the relative proportions of the ethnic groups of newborns as identified by the church recorders: when both parents were listed, the

Table 1. Native Births by Attributed Ethnic Group at Selected Settlements on the Northern Alaska Peninsula to 1897, as Recorded by the Russian Church. [a]

| Ethnic Attribution | PACIFIC COAST | | | BERING SEA SLOPE | | | | | | |
| | Katmai | | Ugashik | | Severnovsk | | Egegik | | Paugvik | |
	no.	%	no.	%	no.	%	no.	%	no.	%
"Aleut"	129	100.0	343	89.1	148	93.7	12	14.8	12	2.7
Aglurmiut			26	6.8	4	2.5	64	79.0	393	87.3
Kiatiirmiut			2	0.5	4	2.5			6	1.3
Kusquqvagmiut			14	3.6	2	1.3	5	6.2	39	8.7
Total numbers	129		385		158		81		450	

a From Alaska Russian Church (1816-1936). Figures for the Bering Sea slope include all available non-Creole births from Nushagak mission records from the earliest recorded through 1897; those for Katmai include only those from Kodiak mission records for years in which the settlement is set out with separate headings (hence the more modest sample).

ethnic group was that of the father; when no father was shown, it was that of the mother. As both Aglurmiut and Kusquqvagmiut stemmed from the same general (Kuskokwim River) region, the two can reasonably be viewed and counted as relative intruders into the Naknek drainage. Although both "Aleut" and Kiatiirmiut together represent older inhabitants of the region around the Naknek River, suggesting that they, too, might be combined, these two were nevertheless of differing language groups — Kiatiirmiut, like Kusqukqagmiut and Aglurmiut, speaking versions of Central Yupik, "Aleut" speaking Alutiiq. In any event, Paugvik and the Severnovsk settlements are visibly at opposite poles, the former with some 95% of the people recorded as Aglurmiut-Kuskukvagmiut, less than 3% "Aleut" or Alutiiq; in the Severnovsk settlements the reverse holds, nearly 94% Alutiiq, the other three barely totaling 6%. Thus, overall differences in ascribed origin are unmistakable In addition to the Paugvik and the Severnovsk settlements, of major interest here, it is evident that Ugashik was still in great majority Alutiiq (nearly 90%), whereas Egegik was about 85% Aglurmiut-Kusquqvagmiut.

Second, because the attributions are heavily those of the fathers of the newborn, the table provides a hint of the frequency of men's marriage into communities in which they were ethnic outsiders. It must be noted that these figures include births recorded well into the 1890s, by which time some population dispersal and amalgamation had certainly occurred under Russian and then American administration of the region.

A possibly more significant detail is that although in the Severnovsk settlements there were births ascribed to Kusquqvagmiut and Kiatiirmiut before 1870, there were no Aglurmiut births recorded until after that date — a suggestion that the enmity between the upper and lower Naknek drainage people was slow to be overcome.

Settlements and Population

In addition to the maintenance of vital statistics records, Russian priests were also charged with annual visits to villages under their jurisdiction and the maintenance of annual confessional registers for each settlement. These registers were intended to include a listing by name of all residents of a settlement, with an assigned age for all persons, and an indication of whether they had confessed. Non-baptized and apostate persons were also to be reported, although it is pretty obvious that they fairly consistently were not. Through the course of the nineteenth century the numbers of conversions, hence of confessants, grew until at least by the latter part of the century the confessional registers must have included the total Native population. Table 2 presents totals derived from these church records at intervals from 1850 to 1880, to which

Table 2. Enumerated Native Population of the Naknek Drainage, 1850-1910

	COAST[a]				INTERIOR[b]			DRAINAGE REGION
Date	Male	Female	Total		Male	Female	Total	Total
Confessional Registers								
1850	72	87	159		48	51	99	258
1860	95	67	192		36	31	67	259
1868[c]	62	68	130		31	32	62	193
1880	113	89	202		59	58	117	319
U.S. Census Records								
1880			192				162	354
1890	67	69	136		47	47	94	230
1900	70	61	131		54	46	100	231
1910	59	57	116		37	37	74	190

a Includes the village of Paugvik all years, Kinuyak in 1890, Natives of Naknek in 1900, 1910.
b Includes villages listed variously as Severnovsk, Ikhak, Ikkhagmiut, Nunamiut, Kanigmiut.
c For a few years after the U.S. purchase of Alaska in 1867 there are no church records.
Sources: Confessional registers: Alaska Russian Church (1733-1938, Nushagak); U.S. Census: 1880, Petroff (1884); 1890, Porter (1893); 1900, 1910, microfilm of original enumeration records, U.S. Census, U.S. National Archives. Adapted from Dumond (1986:Table 5).

are added totals from the U.S. censuses from 1880 (the first) to 1910, which of course was the last before the volcanic eruption of 1912.

As the notes to Table 2 imply, over the course of the nineteenth century the locations, or at least the designations, of some of the settlements in the drainage changed. In especial reference to Severnovsk settlements the earliest mention, as already described, is of Severnovsk "Aleuts" in the vital statistics records of the Unalaska mission for 1827-28. In 1841 a similar reference indicates that 46 Severnovsk individuals had been baptized by a priest from Kodiak, and in 1847 some 15 additional Severnovsk people were listed as baptized by the priest from Nushagak. Thereafter, both vital statistics and confessional registers of the Nushagak mission refer either to Severnovsk Aleuts or to Severnovsk settlements with regularity, although not yearly.

From 1850 through the 1860s, mission references are to two Severnovsk villages, which are designated simply as the first and second Severnovsk settlements. Beginning in the early 1870s, however, there are references only to a single Severnovsk village — or at least settle-ments one and two are not specifically referred to. In 1877 the first reference to "Severnovsk Aleuts in Ikkhagmiut village" appears, and for more than 20 years therafter the village of Ikkhagmiut (sometimes written Ikakhmiut) is listed alone. The 1880 U.S. census specifies a

single permanent settlement, Ikkhagmiut, in the area.

Regarding Ikkhagmiut, the priest who included it in his rounds in 1895 indicated it to be *rather sizeable in number of barabaras; the residents here are all Aleuts, they live very industriously; here there are still many furbearers in the mountains and forests: caribou, bears, foxes, beaver, etc. They sell their catch much more dearly than those living near Nushagak, since they trade not with... the Nushagak agent ... but with an agent of the Kodiak district. In the settlement itself there is no store, which for the local residents has the same significance as a tavern for Russian commoners [i.e., as a source of strong drink]. The barabaras of all are fairly clean, light; nearly every householder has his own baidarka. The women dress entirely in the... Great Russian manner: all have sarafans and sleeveless jackets. The chapel here was built of logs in 1879 [1877 according to other sources], in the name of the Kazan ikon of the Mother of God. At present it is becoming dilapidated. Its interior is not large, there are not many ikons, but some of the ikons they do have are in silver mountings.* [5]

Nevertheless, the absence of a specific reference to a second settlement may not indicate the absence of such a settlement. For in 1898 the priest, Father Vladimir Modestov, reported:

I went to upper Severnovsk settlement or out-settlement, 10 miles distant from

Severnovsk settlement. The residents of this out-settlement at the arrival of a priest always come to Severnovsk settlement for confession and communion. Now I went there first to give communion to a dying woman and second to bless the houses with holy water.... Having given communion to the dying woman, I held a prayer service... and blessed the houses...; in all there are 6 houses here. [6]

An earlier comment (of 1889) regarding the existence of a second Severnovsk village is in the account of an English visitor to the area, to be described in a later section of this chapter.

In 1900 the church vital statistics records refer both to "Severnovsk Aleuts" and to "Kanigmiut Aleuts" (the 1900 U.S. census makes no clear reference by village name). This continues in vital statistics in 1903 with "Severnovsk settlement" alongside "Kanigmiut settlement." In 1904 the confessional register lists Ikkhagmiut and Kanigmiut. In 1905 vital statistics entries contain the last reference to Ikkhagmiut, also listing Kanigmiut and adding another settlement, Nunamiut. From that time until 1911 references in all records are only to Severnovsk Nunamiut settlement and Severnovsk Kanigmiut settlement, where in 1911 the combined population of confessants was reportedly 91. Finally, according to a list of Orthodox chapels made in 1919, it had been the settlement of Nunamiut that contained the chapel dedicated to Our Lady of Kazan at the time of the volcanic eruption of 1912 and the abandonment of the Severnovsk settlements. A chapel similarly dedicated was installed at the new, down-river settlement the survivors established after the eruption.

Although the 1905 reference to Ikkhagmiut along with the other two might suggest that the Ikkhagmiut settlement

Figure 42 – The chapel at Nunamiut, the main Severnovsk settlement abandoned in 1912. Photo in 1919 by W.L. Henning, National Geographic Katmai Expeditions, courtesy of Archives and Manuscripts Department, University of Alaska Anchorage.

had been abandoned and superceded by one of the others, presumably Nunamiut, available evidence seems to point to another conclusion. For the confessional register for 1878 indicates that a chapel to the Virgin of Kazan was present in Ikkhagmiut and the register of the following year indicates that it was built of logs, but the register for 1896 indicates that the chapel in the Nunamiut settlement dedicated to Our Lady of Kazan had been built of logs in 1877. This seems to mean that Ikkhagmiut was simply renamed, despite the reference to both Ikkhagmiut and Nunamiut in vital statistics entries in 1905. The church and clergy register for 1910 confirms the presence at Nunamiut of the chapel to Our Lady of Kazan, built in 1877, while also adding that a second chapel had been built in 1902 at Kanigmiut, dedicated to Nikolai the Miracleworker. [7]

Just where were these settlements? From its name it seems certain enough that Ikkhagmiut must have been very close to the Ikkhak or Ikak River (now the Ukak), which flows into Iliuk Arm of Naknek Lake immediately south of the outlet of the Savonoski River. The historically known "Savonoski" village that was abandoned in 1912, which contained the chapel and in at least its last incarnation was referred to as Nunamiut, is located on the bank of the Savonoski River about a mile upstream from the Ukak mouth. Kanigmiut, in view of information gained in several attempts at archaeological reconnaissance, must have been at or near the mouth of the Grosvenor River, which drains Grosvenor Lake into the Savonoski River close to ten

Albatross -Alaska-1900
Bristol Bay Dist.

Figure 43 – The Native village west of the Naknek Packing Co., north side of the Naknek River, in 1900. Fish and Wildlife photo No. 22-FFA-2546, U.S. National Archives.

miles above the mouth of the latter. According to nineteenth century maps (as, that of Vasil'ev, illustrated above) that same spot must have been the approximate location of the earlier Alinnak. In short, Nunamiut and Ikkhagmiut, whether one or two settlements, was or were close to the mouths of the Ukak and Savonoski rivers, whereas Kanigmiut and Alinnak were apparently close to the confluence of the Grosvenor with the Savonoski.

Although occupation in the portion of Paugvik that we excavated in 1961, 1973, and 1985 was described above as having ended not later than about 1870, note a to Table 2 shows the name Paugvik as being in use later than that. Solving the contradiction requires the unscrambling of clues in various historical documents.

Describing a visit in the early 1870s H. W. Elliott remarked that a "deserted settlement — ruins of Paugwik" was visible at the mouth of the Naknek River, while Native people were living in an "adjoining village," which he however did not name.[8] The early twentieth-century church records list both Paugvik and Naknek ("Nak-Nik") as settlements, and the U.S. censuses of 1900 and 1910 also list both Paugvik (or some variation of that name) and Naknek. The 1910 U.S. census also showed the Norwegian immigrant Martin Monsen to be living in Paugvik. Now the riddle begins to clear with a report by the archaeologist Helge Larsen of the visit he made to the area in 1948. Larsen was told by Monsen that the old village of the archaeological excavations had been abandoned for some

20 years in 1895 when he (Monsen) had moved to Naknek (not Paugvik) on the north bank of the river. This leaves us to presume that for purposes of the U.S. census the newer Naknek settlement actually retained the older Paugvik name even though the population had shifted upstream to a point closer to the fish processing plant of the Naknek Packing Co. that was established in the 1890s.[9]

And what of "Nak-Nik"? As indicated in discussion of the earliest map, in 1818 the settlement across the Naknek River mouth from Paugvik was shown as *Kougumik*, although church records thereafter appear to include the entire population at the river mouth as people of Paugvik. This continued until 1890, when the cross-river settlement of Kinuyak is listed, together with both Paugvik and Naknek. Finally, a reasonably definitive answer is indicated in a map made by topographer W. S. Post, who accompanied the geologist J. E. Spurr on his geological explorations in 1898, as will be described in a later section. The contour map of that date of a portion of Bristol Bay indicates a single settlement "Pawik" on the north bank, and the settlement of "Naknik" directly across the river on the south shore (see Figure 46, page 77).[10] For the 1900 and 1910 US censuses, then — and probably also the concurrent church registers — it can only be presumed that Nak-Nik or Naknek designates the village south of the river, now South Naknek, while Paugvik refers to the village north of the river, now Naknek.

With the arrival of more Russian priests in Alaska, the emphasis on conversions went on apace. The endeavor was not without trouble for the missionaries, of course, for the process of eradicating some predilections that obviously were of long standing among the Native population was not an easy one. In the nineteenth century there are numerous complaints about recalcitrance on the part of local people. As one priest serving the Nushagak mission in the 1860s characterized many of his charges,

They do not abandon shamanism; they live unmarried, begetting children; they abandon the wenches to live in poverty even with children; they train their children neither to any obedience nor to any occupations, nor to gratitude; and some pander their own wives and give them to others; even against the will of the wives themselves they force them to bear violations; and the very greatest outrage for me, and I do not doubt to say for God as well, is rendered by those of them who on various empty pretexts taik themselves out of listening to a sermon.

The Severnovsk people, however, seemed better in at least some of these regards, for "due to the remoteness of these . . . settlements from the Kiatiirmiut and Kusquqvagmiut, shamans do not come to them and no one has summoned one . . . in a long time." Nevertheless, "fathers and mothers regret to release their daughters in marriage to Katmai or to Paugvik, likewise other Aglurmiut or Aleuts do not move to them to live. From this, marriages among them often are with kin or [between individuals] of entirely unequal ages." [11]

One must suppose that the population increase shown on Table 2 as having taken place between 1850 and 1880 was owed in significant part, perhaps entirely, to continued conversions, which by the latter year must have included essentially the entire Native population of the region. Although the figures in the 1880 U.S. census were derived largely from church records rather than from a count by the census taker (Petroff 1884:v), the totals differ somewhat from those taken here from copies of the confessional records (which list more people at Paugvik and fewer at Severnovsk than does the U.S. census); the reason for this is unknown. In any event, when population totals shown in the U.S. census shrink after 1880, it is reasonable to think that the decline was not owed to conversions having dwindled, but was real.

This supposition has been supported by an earlier study in which the 1880 confessional totals were combined with the records of births and deaths also maintained by the church. From it I concluded two things: The first of these is that the population of the Naknek drainage area was in fact shrinking from early in the nineteenth century and the establishment of Russian control, in a decline that amounted on average to more than one percent per year, at a rate that would have served to reduce the population by as much as 50% within about 50 years. The second and related conclusion, even using some slightly less severe assumptions, was that the population at 1800 was at least three times the size of the population enumerated in 1900. [12]

Although it can be shown from church records that there was a significant movement of people in both directions between the Severnovsk settlements and related Alutiiq villages of Shelikof Strait (Douglas and Katmai), and it is certainly probable that the same situation existed between Paugvik and other Aglurmiut settlements around Bristol Bay, [13] it can be supposed that out- and in-migrations approximately balanced one another throughout the nineteenth century. The implication here is that some factor other than migration was responsible for the population decline.

And in fact this shrinkage must have been quite irregular, if looked at year by year. The available church vital statistics documents indicate that the Naknek region in the years 1853, 1859, 1860, 1863, 1882, 1883, 1887, 1888, 1889, 1890, and 1891 experienced deaths higher than average as a result of unnamed "epidemics," of sicknesses characterized by stabbing chest pains, coughs, blood spitting, lung disease of unspecified nature, or of identified influenza. Although the rate of identified tuberculosis was also increasing through time, deaths from it were not concentrated by year. In short, the major cause of the population decline appears to have been recurrent respiratory diseases such as influenza, often as epidemics. [14]

And as will be seen, the nineteenth century did not see the last of major epidemics of respiratory diseases that took such a toll on the people of the Naknek drainage region.

Households and Families

In addition to total population numbers, confessional registers for some years include information that can be used to estimate family size and at least to some extent household size. That is, in these particular registers, households were to be numbered serially, with the male household head appearing first, followed by his wife and his unmarried children, then by married children with their listed offspring. From this information it is possible to conclude that in 1880 in Paugvik there were fifteen separate households providing homes to slightly more than 40 different married couples or families with a total population of about 200 people. At the same time, in the Severnovsk settlement there were seventeen apparently separate households providing shelter for 27 families and 117 people — amounting only to about half as many people per household (less than seven persons) as in Paugvik (more than thirteen persons). [15] This seems in accord with the description of the major Severnovsk settlement given by Father Modestov, quoted in the previous section of this chapter.

There is also a special social factor relating to housing practices that needs be considered at this point. At Paugvik, according to some historical references (one of which follows in a later section), there was a so-called "kashim" (kazhim according to the Russians) or special large structure in which ceremonial occasions were celebrated. Reports indicate that in Paugvik, as among Yupik people farther north, this structure also functioned as a men's house — an actual residence where young and middle-aged men spent most of their time, while their wives maintained the separated family house.[16] Such a split living arrangement, with its men's dormitory, must have effectively lessened the number of persons actually living in the 15 households of the confessional register. The same factor seems not to have existed at the Severnovsk settlements. Although Father Modestov mentioned the presence of a kashim at the major Severnovsk village, there is no indication that it functioned as a special men's house; indeed, it seems doubtful that kashims ever functioned in this way among Alutiiq people, serving instead for purely ceremonial functions.[17] If this is the case, Alutiiq families would expectedly be living all together more often, with the household sizes as given being reasonably accurate.

Social factors in housing aside, Ivan Petroff, the compiler in 1880 of the first U.S. census of Alaska, furnished a comment that describes the houses themselves. On the treeless coast, he said, *the houses ... may be described as follows: A circular mound of earth, grass-grown and littered with all sorts of household utensils, a small spiral coil of smoke rising from the apex .... The entrance ... is a low, irregular, square aperture, through which the inmate stoops and passes down a foot or two through a short, low, passage onto the earthen floor within. The interior generally consists of an irregularly-shaped square or circle twelve or fifteen or twenty feet in diameter, receiving its only light from without through the small smoke-opening at the apex of the roof .... The fire-place is*

directly under this opening .... [B]eds or couches of skins and grass mats are laid, slightly raised above the floor, upon... frames made of sticks and saplings or rough-hewn planks ....

This description could reasonably be applied to the houses we excavated at the Paugvik site, an area somewhat removed from even small stands of timber at the present day. But more toward the interior, Petroff said, *where both fuel and building material are more abundant, the houses change somewhat in appearance and construction; the excavation of the coast houses, made for the purpose of saving both articles just mentioned, disappears and gives way to log structures above the ground, but still covered with sod. Living within convenient distance of timber, the people here do not depend so much upon the natural warmth of mother earth.*

This greater access to standing timber would have been the case at the Severnovsk settlements, in an area into which spruce had migrated several centuries before the arrival of the Russians, and in which birch and willow trees had been plentiful much earlier than that. Although the multiroom houses along the lower Savonoski River that seem to be attributable to the Brooks River Bluffs phase (AD 1350 – 1800) were semi-subterranean like contemporary houses at Brooks River and along the Naknek River, houses occupied in the early twentieth century before the great volcanic eruption were different. As described in the preceding chapter, they were of a single room, less deeply set in the ground, and provided with a window in at least one wall, with rectangular floors measuring some 10 by 12 feet Altogether, these seem appropriate for smaller household groups such as the confessional-register census indicates. [18]

It was into a home like this at the Severnovsk settlement of Ikkhagmiut that the baby Pelagiya was born to Vasiliy Ityg'yuk and his wife Mariya in 1879, although her birth was not recorded until 1881, presumably because the priest did not visit sooner. At the time, the family included Pelagiya's three older brothers and three sisters. She would be much later known as Pelagiya (or Pelagia) Melgenak. [19] Her story will be resumed later.

Visitors

Numerous references to visits by Russian Orthodox priests to Naknek region settlements have been made in earlier pages. Paugvik, as an important village on Bristol Bay, was visited virtually every year and is included in confessional registers. The Severnovsk settlements, on the other hand, were visited much less frequently by the circuit-traveling priests, despite the theoretical expectation that they would make visits at least annually. Although gaps in surviving church records suggest that the collection is not complete, those available do make it clear that in many years visits to the upper end of Naknek Lake were not feasible. Indeed, for the 63-year period from 1847, when a Nushagak priest first visited, through 1909, the apparent last visit before the eruption, existing records indicate that the Severnovsk villages were called on only 24

times. Little wonder, then, that some priests could complain that *debauchery, illicit cohabitation, giving girls to husbands before marriage, and changing of such brides and grooms, [and] cohabitation with close kin are particularly developed.... The reason for this is that they are especially remote from their priest... and even from their own Native fellow-tribesmen.... Their communications are with settlements of the Kodiak parish — Katmai and Douglas, as the closest — a day or at most two days' travel.... In other settlements of the mission, if there is some vice or some crime is committed by someone, the toyon, even if he wished to hide this from the priest, is afraid that the toyons or residents of nearby settlements will communicate about this to the priest.... Therefore, all the toyons everywhere communicate to the priest candidly both the good and the bad. In Severnovsk settlement, remote from the priest..., it is just the opposite — everything is carefully hidden.* [20]

By the latter part of the nineteenth century and the period under American control, however, times had somewhat changed. A number of visiting outlanders left at least brief written references to their travels through the Naknek region. In most cases, these focused especially on the traverse between Bristol Bay and the Pacific by way of Katmai Pass.

Ivan Petroff –

The first U.S. census of Alaska was officially authorized on April 20, 1880; on the following day Russian-born Ivan Petroff was on his way from Washington D.C. to San Francisco as duly appointed agent, and three weeks later he arrived in Unalaska. Thereafter, he reported visits (largely by skin boat) to the Pribilof Islands, to the Shumagins, to St. Michael on the Bering Sea; he logged travel along portions of the Yukon and a descent of the Kuskokwim. In September he arrived at Nushagak, and by the end of that month at the mouth of the Naknek River, where he recorded "Paugwik (2 villages)."

Unfortunately, he left no description of settlements as he moved along. On October 2 he reached the extreme head of Naknek Lake — which, alleging it to be nameless, he christened "Lake Walker" after the then-supervisor of the census. The village at the extreme end of the lake he showed on his map as "Ik-khagmute," again without describing it. He also mapped a second settlement farther southwest on the lake, which he did not name but of which he did make some brief remarks, as will be seen.

Despite his admission that he acquired most of his regional census data from Russian Church records, Petroff mistook the ethnic divisions of the Native peoples that are so unmistakably indicated in those records, as well as elements of local history that must have been related to him. For he assigned both Paugvik and the "Lake Walker" settlements to "Aglemute," or Aglurmiut people. That he had been provided with a more accurate history of events, however, is revealed by his assertion that *in former times there existed another element among the Aglemute — Aleutian invaders, who for some time inhabited two settlements on the mouth of the Naknek river. As far as can be ascertained, the Aleutians retreated down the peninsula as far as Oogashik at the beginning of the present century.*

This he had backwards, of course, for the historic Aglurmiut were the invaders, and the earlier-resident "Aleutian" or Alutiiq people had retreated from them not only to Ugashik, but to the upper end of Naknek Lake. And it was no doubt partly in memory of former hostilities that the people of "Lake Walker," as Petroff also reported, were accustomed to go "down to Katmai to do their shopping…, undertaking a very fatiguing tramp over mountains and glaciers… in preference to the canoe journey to the Bristol Bay stations."[21] That is, as late as 1880 the Alutiiq people still preferred to deal with other Alutiit.

Somewhat more colorful descriptions of the lake area are provided in newspaper interviews regarding Petroff's trip. There, his "Lake Walker" is described as *some ninety miles in length and varying in width from five to fifteen miles, irregular in its contours…. The scenery around this inland sea displays to the delighted traveler all variations from rolling moorland to wooded uplands, rocky cliffs, and… the grandest Alpine scenery….*

At the eastern extremity of this large inland water a section of it is almost separated by a dam of mountains, communicating with the main body by a gap of less than half a mile in width. Stupendous heights surround this nook, rising almost perpendicularly from the surface and reaching far into the clouds. In this confined, funnel-like basin, the winds and squalls hold constant carnival.... At the western end of this lakelet a numerous party of natives were engaged in fishing just below a waterfall of considerable height.... A village was formerly located here, and a legend is transmitted that once in times gone by the whole population was killed by a marauding party of Aleuts, who surprised the settlement in the dead of night. The tale was told by one survivor who hid himself under the waterfall, and thus escaped the enemy.

Although this camp is evidently the second, and unnamed, "Lake Walker" village shown on the map of his official report, the wording implies that the settlement was seasonal. The "legend" he mentioned gives further evidence of former hostility between Aglurmiut of Paugvik and Alutiit of the Severnovsk settlements. That is, downstream Aglurmiut (Petroff's "natives") had evidently established a camp or even a more permanent settlement near a waterfall, presumably the one in the midsection of Brooks River, which was then attacked by Severnovsk people ("Aleuts").

Figure 44 – View of Iliuk Arm of "Lake Walker" (i.e., Naknek Lake) and "Mt. Kakhtolinat," according to Ivan Petroff (1884, facing page 24). Compare this cozy nook with the photograph of the same area on the present title page.

73

From Ikkhagmiut, Petroff's hike across Katmai Pass to Katmai village was uneventful. And on October 19 he was transported — again by skin boat — across Shelikof Strait to Kodiak, from where he was able to obtain passage south. [22]

The Earl of Lonsdale –

Hugh Cecil Lowther, Fifth Earl of Lonsdale — spendthrift, official heir to one of Britain's richest estates, and avid sportsman — left England in February 1888, bound for Canada and an arctic adventure, the trip apparently related to dalliance with an actress that had resulted in an illegitimate child, a lurid lawsuit, and possibly a reprimand from Queen Victoria. Bankrolled in part by the *New York Herald* and able to draw as a further bank on resources of the Hudson Bay Company, the errant patrician entrained to a point west of Winnipeg, from where he began a great, nearly year-long trek by dogsled and boat, first hopping from post to post of the Hudson Bay Company down the Mackenzie River to the arctic coast, then west along the Yukon to Alaska and the Bering Sea, and overland to Nushagak, where he rested a short time. From Nushagak he and his party sledded to Koggiung and finally to Paugvik — called "Packwick" in his diary and in regular letters to his wife — where they arrived on January 31, 1889. Despite near-daily entries in his diary and letters carrying lengthy descriptions of events of travel, there is almost no description of villages or of Native people, whom he obviously looked down on — and consistently referred to as "Indians," no matter where he met them. He did purchase a number of photographs of places, and he carried a camera with which he made occasional photographs himself.

With guides and other sleds added at Paugvik, the party that left on February 1 to move up the ice of the Naknek River consisted of eight sleds, 68 dogs, and 18

Figure 45 – The Lonsdale party moving toward Katmai Pass, 1889 (original print copied by permission of the seventh Earl of Lonsdale), Copyright The Trustees of the British Museum.

people, counting Lonsdale and one English assistant. Passing up the river and portaging around the rapids that day, they crossed the major part of Naknek Lake on February 2. Although the exact trail they followed, largely along shorelines, is impossible to identify from his description, one comment regarding the party's inability to learn the best route to avoid rotten sections of lake ice, was that the "Packwick & Severnosky Indians don't correspond at all or communicate" with one another.

In any event, by the end of the day of February 3 they were in the "upper lake" (apparently Iliuk Arm), and the following day arrived at "Severnosky," or the main Severnovsk village, where the party was ferried across the Savonoski River on baidarkas, or three-hatched kayaks. Again there is no description of the place, but there is at least a comment indicating the presence of more than a single settlement thereabouts. For finding that the major village was short of fish for the party's dogs, Lonsdale was able to send skin boats "up 20 miles to the next village" for dried fish (which did not arrive, for the river froze and the boats could not return).

So on February 7 the under-provisioned caravan of sleds pushed toward the pass, arriving below it on the second evening. They crossed in a growing storm the following day, only to be caught by the blizzard on the other side. Although the intrepid Lonsdale and the people with three of the sleds made it to Katmai village on February 12, the remaining sled crews holed up in the snow to wait for the storm to blow over; most of their unfed dogs froze to death. Such can be wintertime in Katmai Pass. [23]

The Frank Leslie Alaska Expedition –

In early 1890, the staff of *Frank Leslie's Illustrated Newspaper* hatched a scheme for fairly extensive explorations in Alaska, and in that year and early 1891 a series of parties under the newspaper's sponsorship traveled through various areas of southeast Alaska, then along the Tanana, the Yukon, and the Kuskokwim rivers on the mainland. Two of these parties went from Bristol Bay to Kodiak by way of Katmai Pass. In January 1891 a group led by E. H. Wells went directly by sled from Nushagak to the pass, a trip Wells related almost without describing it, and certainly with no mention of settlements. A. B. Schanz, on the other hand, who was authorized to enumerate village populations for the census (dated retroactively to the previous year, 1890), left Nushagak at the same time as Wells, with trader John Clark. Their sled trip carried them up the Nushagak and Mulchatna rivers, down the Chulitna, to Lake Clark (for which they claimed discovery and which they named), and from there across Iliamna Lake on the ice to Koggiung and down the Kvichak to the mouth of the Naknek. At "Pak Wik" his reception on February 27, Schanz said, "was the most cordial of my whole Alaskan experience. . . . Everything in the village was offered me most liberally" and he slept that night in the kashim "among the fighting-bucks and the fleas."

Like Wells and unlike Lonsdale, Schanz had only minor trouble in Katmai Pass itself, although he ran into problems on the way there. For while they were camped with their dog teams by the river ice "the Nak Nik River broke up from source to mouth" from sudden and unseasonably warm weather, forcing them to break a trail overland to "Lake Nak Nik." Then, after sledding "several days over a wide, uninteresting expanse of ice" they neared "Severnosky village," when *half of my crew and myself... received a cold bath by running in the dark into open water.... We only arrived at Severnosky at ten at night, dripping wet, where we were not frozen stiff, and the natives did everything for us in their power. We remained there the next day to prepare for the trip over the pass, and the natives nursed us with the greatest hospitality.*

Unfortunately, there is no further description of the place as they regrouped to resume travel. After a two-day climb they camped "within sight of the notorious pass... in the last thin little group of trees," where they were held up for a day and a half while a storm blew itself out. Leaving one of their two sleds, and hitching all 23 dogs to the other, they stampeded over the pass and slid down the Pacific side of the mountain, arriving at sea level only eight miles from Katmai village in less than six hours after leaving their enforced camp. [24]

Josiah Edward Spurr –

The first contour map of the immediate Naknek region was the work of the geologist Josiah Spurr and cartographer W. S. Post, who in 1898 made a large swing from Cook Inlet, up the Susitna River, along the Kuskokwim, then to Togiak and Nushagak and finally across the pass to Katmai village. By this time commercial fish processors were working on the lower Naknek River, so that when they reached there on October 11, having crossed Bristol Bay by baidarkas, they lodged at a cannery. Although the territory they paddled through on the river and across Naknek Lake is described, and the "native village of Ikkhagamut, or Savonoski, as it is now commonly called," at least received mention, there was again no description of the place and little of the people. Similarly, the pass was described in physical terms — as wild, rugged, and difficult, flanked by volcanoes and glaciers, where violent winds might blow stones through the air, and with a note that there many people had lost their lives there. One volcano (no name given) was seen to sometimes smoke. Crossing by foot with Native guides, they had no appreciable difficulty in quiet weather, although they felt a slight earthquake as they moved a short way from the pass down the Pacific slope.

There are evidently two editions of maps of the route, both to the same scale. One of them, evidently the earlier, names the lake and river as "Naknik," and locates the settlement of the same name on the south bank of the Naknek River mouth, across from "Pawik." The second, which is bound in the official published report, shows both lake and south-bank settlement as "Naknek." The first of these also shows a

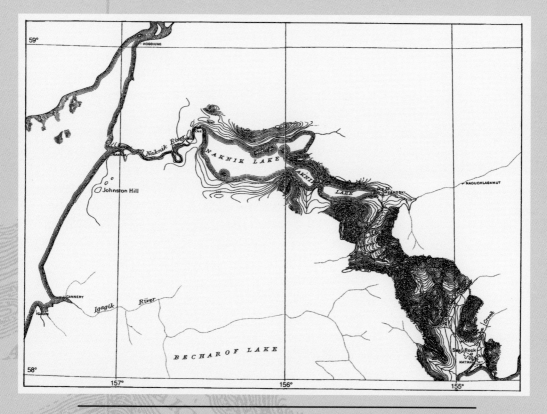

Figure 46 – Map of the crossing of Katmai Pass by Spurr and Post, 1898.

second settlement on what is evidently the Savonoski River, located somewhat less than 20 miles upstream from the village marked "Savonoski," which on both maps appears near the mouth of the river and Iliuk Arm. Not mentioned in the text, this second settlement is labeled "Naouchlagamut," its position approximately that of the settlemenet "Alinnak" on the Vasil'ev map referred to earlier. [25]

Other Travelers –

Earlier in the year of Spurr's travel there had been at least one other crossing of the Alaska Peninsula at Katmai Pass by an outlander. In late fall of 1897 a series of

whaling ships had been frozen in around Point Barrow, and the officer of one of the ships, George Fred Tilton, volunteered to go south as far as a telegraph office in order to inform the ships' owners and request relief. Tilton crossed Katmai Pass to Shelikof Strait and the Pacific in March, evidently leaving no description of places or people, and little of the pass itself, save that the blizzard was almost continuous. [26]

The year 1898 was also the year of the gold strike at what became the town of Nome, and by the beginning of 1899 the rush was on. According to some accounts, written well after the fact, the summer approach to Nome by way of Katmai village, Katmai Pass, and the Naknek region became so popular with gold seekers on their way to Anvil Creek and the Nome gold sands that a "bunk house was constructed at Katmai, and small boats plied Naknek Lake and Naknek River to accommodate the travelers." If this is true, one must expect that the previous isolation of the Severnovsk settlements was wrecked for good. Nevertheless, no contemporary description of the use of the route in this way is known. [27]

A more graphic description of at least part of the route, although nothing of the Naknek region villages or people, was presented by the author Rex Beach, who crossed from Katmai village to the Naknek region early in 1901 on his way to a reported gold strike on the Kuskokwim that turned out to be bogus. Katmai Pass appears both in a personal memoir and in a piece of avowed fiction. In both, however, the only somewhat graphic description applies to the village of Katmai.

At Katmai, Beach said in his memoir, "the ... barabaras were completely covered with earth and sod, the trader's log store was chained down with heavy ship's cables that ran over the roof and were fastened to stout deadmen sunk in the ... ground." Otherwise roofs "had a way of picking themselves up and sailing out to sea when the wind blew," according to the store keeper Petellin, described as fat and cross-eyed. On the under-provisioned trip Beach and a companion, with a single guide and five dogs, were caught by a

storm as they neared pass level; Beach fell suddenly sick and was given a double jolt of brandy to buck him up, which essentially knocked him out. He describes the frightful climb toward the pass and the rise of the wind graphically enough, but the down-grade toward the Severnovsk settlement was evidently invisible to him as he stumbled along behind the sled in a drunken and snowy stew, staggering to stay upright. His blind and selective memory obviously warped his picture of the pass, for in his work of fiction, in which two men attack the pass from the other (Severnovsk) side, there is no description until they make their final assault on the mountain defile, and struggle downward through a storm toward Katmai — which again is described as having a store with cable-anchored roof, and keeper both fat and cross-eyed. [28]

So much for the meeting between the Naknek region and the bigger world around the end of the nineteenth century.

Notes

[1] VanStone (1988: map facing p. 77).

[2] Lütke (1836:Atlas, facing p. 286). From the conformation of the lake and the settlements near it, this Vasil'ev map (of 1831-32) evidently provided the model for another early map that appeared in the Russian edition of Tikhmenev's (1863) history of the Russian American Company. This is reproduced by Solovjova and Vovnyanko (2002:Fig. 36).

[3] Brief test excavations at a site or sites immediately east of Iliuk Arm are reported by Davis (1954). The most definitive recent discussion of the sites on the Savonoski River is by Hilton (2002), although other archaeological surveys of the region were conducted in the 1960s. Details regarding the Naknek River are in Dumond (1981).

[4] The early Russian Church history in the region is succinctly summarized by VanStone (1967:Chapt. 2). The baptism of Katmai and Severnovsk people is reported in Alaska Russian Church (1816-1936, Kodiak, 1841), the assignment of the three settlements to the Nushagak Mission in Alaska Russian Church (1733-1938, Nushagak, letter from Bishop of Kamchatka to Missionary of Nushagak Church, July 14, 1844).

[5] Alaska Russian Church (1733 - 1938, Nushagak church service registers, 1 July - 31 December, 1895), translation by Katherine Arndt. Of the specialized references, barabara designates a semisubterranean Native habitation; a baidarka was a kayak, although often with two or three hatches rather than a single one; and the sarafan was a sleeveless gown of Russian style.

[6] Alaska Russian Church (1733 - 1938, Nushagak church service registers, 1 January - 31 December, 1898), translation by Katherine Arndt.

[7] Alaska Russian Church (1733 - 1938, Nushagak, church/clergy registers, dates as given in the text); this information was generously furnished by Katherine Arndt.

[8] Elliott (1886:400).

[9] The listing of M. Monsen is in the original census enumeration sheet for "Bugorwik" (Paugvik), family entry 79. The Larsen account is in Larsen (1950).

[10] Spurr and Post (1898:Map 4).

[11] Alaska Russian Church (1733 - 1938, Nushagak and Bristol Bay travel journals, journal of Hieromonk Feofil Uspenskii, 1865), for which I am grateful to Katherine Arndt.

[12] This study is presented in Dumond (1986: Table 11); the present Table 2 is adapted from Table 5 in that report. Church confessional registers are those of Alaska Russian Church (1733-1938), the records of births, marriages, and deaths are in Alaska Russian Church 1816 - 1936), both available on microfilm held by the University of Alaska Fairbanks, the University of Alaska Anchorage, and the Alaska State Library.

[13] This is based both on interviews in recent years and on examination of Russian Church records, which indicate that some coastal families had their roots in the Severnovsk region in the mid-nineteenth century, and that some Severnovsk families had moved to the interior from the same coast. Similar, but less complete, evidence relates to Paugvik and other settlements of Aglurmiut or Kuskukvagmiut people.

[14] Dumond (1986), in which the existence of the decline is supported by calculated life tables.

[15] The documentary information for this (1880 confessional registers) was also used to produce Table 6 of Dumond (1986), in which I assumed the household enumerations to be correct, although in the present reexamination it was recognized that the Severnovsk settlement included 17 potential households, rather than the 15 erroneously listed in that Table 6. There is a possible further problem with these data, however, in that the recorders may not have filled out the columns of the registry forms in the precise way intended, so that family members not actually living together may appear to be in a single household. Specifically, the heading of the left hand column of the form calls for it to contain serial numbers of households, with the next

two columns to the right to contain serial numbers for males and females respectively, counting through the entire document. From comparisons of entries in forms for the same families over several decades, however, it seems that some families with a number of married sons grew so large it is hard to imagine them living within a single house, despite the fact that they are listed beside a single household number. One is thus led to suspect that in some cases a single "household" entry may in fact have come to refer to nearby households of related individuals.

[16] See the reference in the succeeding section on the expedition of the Frank Leslie Illustrated Weekly. The reference there to the Paugvik kashim and the men in it was confirmed by an interview in the Naknek area in the 1970s, revealing a memory that in the first decade of the twentieth century a male child spent his time with his father and grandfather in the kashim, and that his mother would bring food to them, approaching only close enough to set it inside the door. During excavations in 1985 we identified the remnant of one large semisubterranean structure at Paugvik as a probable kashim, although for various reasons it was not excavated.

[17] Father Modestov's comment relates to events of January 31, 1897, in his church service register for that year (Alaska Russian Church 1733 - 1938, Nushagak); see D. W. Clark (1984:193), with some other references for kashims in Alutiiq villages.

[18] The description quoted is from Petroff (1884:15). Davis (1954:66, Fig. 15) describes the houses at the Severnovsk ("Old Savonoski") site that were in use immediately before the eruption.

[19] The birth is recorded in Alaska Russian Church (1816-1936, Nushagak, 1881). Although the Vasiliy Ityg'yuk family is not listed in the 1880 confessional register, presumably through error, it is included in registers of the late 1870s and others of the early 1880s (Alaska Russian Church 1733-1938, Nushagak, e.g., 1876, 1884). The parents were reported to be aged about 47-48 (father), and 38-39 (mother) at the time of the birth of Pelagiya — a name which has been spelled variously in English as Pelegeia, Pelagia, Pelagiia, Pelekai, and probably other ways.

[20] Alaska Russian Church (1733 - 1938, Nushagak church service register, 1 January - 31 December 1897, Vladimir Modestov); translation courtesy of Katherine Arndt.

[21] The longer quotation is from Petroff (1884:136), the shorter from page 24 of the same source, with other details from page 25 as well as from the New York Herald story referenced in the following note.

[22] Most of the actual travel details are from "Alaska's Census," a story in two parts that appeared in the New York Herald newspaper on January 10 and 11, 1881, with the present direct quotation from the second installment. The account of the attack by "Aleuts" is repeated in the official report (Petroff 1884:24), and can only have referred to one of two streams that feed into the lake near the western end of Iliuk Arm — Margo Creek, in which the high falls is a permanent barrier to salmon, and fish-rich Brooks River, with its lower falls, which is much more likely the place meant. Petroff was responsible for much of H. H. Bancroft's History of Alaska, and although his veracity has been called seriously into question with regard to a number of his writings, his report for the 1880 census (Petroff 1884) is generally accepted as accurate (see Pierce 1968, with additional references).

[23] A thorough account of the adventure based on Lonsdale's diaries and letters, as well as a description and analysis of the large British Museum collection of objects that he obtained from Native people along his way, is provided by Krech (1989). Additional details cited here are from parts of the diaries and letters that were edited out of the published version, and to which with the collection of the fifth Earl's photos I was graciously allowed access in 1977 by the seventh Earl of Lonsdale: The party departing Paugvik is enumerated in the diary entry for January 31, while the remark about the lack of communication between Paugvik and Severnovsk people is

Katmai caldera and hanging glacier, photo by Keith Trexler, 1972.

from the diary entry of February 3. Comments about a second village near the main Severnovsk settlement (the latter evidently Ikkhagmiut) appear in the diary entry for Febuary 6, and in the text of a letter to Lady Lonsdale dated the same.

[24] The narratives of participants in the expedition are serialized in issues of Frank Leslie's Illustrated Newspaper between June 20 and November 28, 1891. The portions of the accounts of Wells and of Schanz that detail their travel through the Naknek region appeared on September 19 and November 28, respectively, with all quotations from the latter.

[25] The official report is that of Spurr (1900), from which the few direct quotations were taken; somewhat more detail of the travel, however, is in Spurr (1950). The earlier edition of the map (Spurr and Post 1898) was consulted in the U.S. National Archives in Washington, DC.

[26] His account is in Tilton (1928). Although he was successful in getting his message through, bringing supplies when the ice went out the following summer, the situation of the stranded whaling crews also brought the so-called Overland Expedition of 1897-98, in which Lt. D. H. Jarvis, of the Revenue Cutter Service, captained the gathering of a reindeer herd on the Seward Peninsula and a drive to Barrow, arriving in March 1898 with meat on the hoof for the stranded crews (see Bixby 1965:153-191).

[27] The situation as described is summarized in some detail by Hussey (1971:300-303), based in part on Griggs (1922:267).

[28] The personal memoir, with an evidently updated reminiscence, is Beach (1940:61-68), the work of fiction Beach (1909:74-83).

When the Century Turned

Fish Business

The first salmon cannery in the Bristol Bay area was established on the lower Nushagak River in 1884, and at the end of that decade three canneries were operating in the vicinity. In 1890, newly arrived outsiders established salteries on each bank of the Naknek River near its mouth, although both were absorbed by canneries that began active operations in 1895 — on the south by the Alaska Packers Association's Arctic Packing Co. at what is now South Naknek, on the north by the somewhat smaller Naknek Packing Co. in what is now Naknek. By the season of 1900 the output of the Naknek River canneries had increased almost tenfold, and they employed a total of 486 people, including 271 Chinese and 31 local Natives.

By 1905 cannery output had doubled again, with 60 Natives employed in the Naknek canneries, and at least that many more in canneries near the mouth of the Kvichak River a short distance to the north. In 1909 output was three times that of 1900, and thereafter, although the size of the pack fluctuated from year to year it did not significantly decrease in the Naknek-Kvichak area, despite the massive volcanic eruption that would shortly occur. Thus, although the employment opportunities for local Native people increased slowly at first, by the end of the first decade of the twentieth century such opportunities were by no means insignificant.

By this time, it was common for much of the Native population, many of whom were accustomed to spend the summer season in tents and to move from place to place for fishing and hunting, to cluster around the canneries in the hope of jobs as the commercial season began. As will be seen, this was evidently true of people from the Severnovsk settlements as well as those of the lower river. [1]

Albatross -Alaska-1900
Bristol Bay Dist.

Plant of Naknek Packing Co.

Naknek River.

view from ...

A 2544

Figure 47 – The plant of the Naknek Packing Co. of 1900, in what is now the village of Naknek. Fish and Wildlife photo no. 22-FFA-2544, U.S. National Archives.

Figure 48 – Tents of Native people along the Naknek River. Photo in 1919 by E.C. Kolb, National Geographic Society Katmai Expeditions, courtesy Archives and Manuscripts Department, University of Alaska Anchorage.

The Latest Great Eruption

On June 6, 1912, the beginning of the earth's most massive volcanic eruption of the twentieth century was triggered immediately beside Katmai Pass. Magma that underground had a volume of less than three cubic miles was blown out and expanded with air bubbles to create almost seven cubic miles of airborne pumice. From its newly opened vent, called Novarupta, a pyroclastic flow of sand-sized particles swept northwestward for some twelve miles, filling the valley of the major tributaries of the Ukak River to a depth of a thousand feet, reaching the bank of the Ukak itself immediately southeast of Mt. Katolinat. From the time the explosive plume was first sighted by a ship in Shelikof Strait at about 1:00 p.m., June 6, violent expulsions of pumice lasted continuously for nearly three days,

creating columns of dust and ash thousands of feet high, blown eastward over Kodiak Island and ultimately dispersed around the world at high altitude.

Most accounts indicate that there was also a series of earthquake jolts in the week before the actual eruption began. In those first six days of the real event (June 6 to 11), there were daily quakes exceeding 6.0 in magnitude; a more isolated jolt of the same magnitude occurred June 17, and smaller shocks were felt in the Alaska Peninsula region through August of that summer.

East of the eruption site the major fall was recorded from the evening of June 6 through June 9, often accompanied by thunder, lightning, and earthquakes. On downwind Kodiak, buildings were collapsed by the weight of ash a foot or

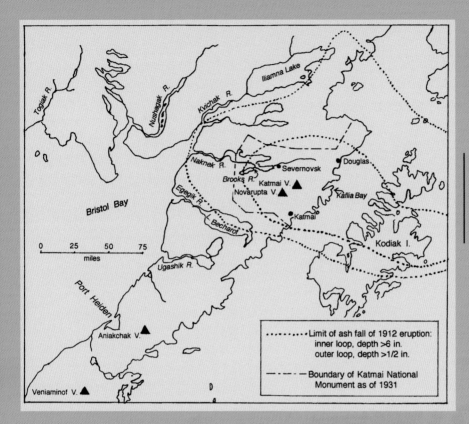

Figure 49 – Area of heavy airfall tephra in June 1912 (based on Griggs 1922).

more in thickness. Because of the wind direction, the lower Naknek River was briefly spared, however. Cannery ships anchored off the river mouth reported that the days of June 6 and 7 were clear on Bristol Bay, but an especially stormy sky appeared June 8, and people from Naknek village reported feeling earthquakes that night. Thereafter, little was noticed before June 12, when dark clouds were seen to the northeast and darkness became general about 9:30 that night, with thunder, lightning, earthquakes, and the beginning of a volcanic ash fall that lasted past midnight, covering surfaces to a depth of an inch or more. It cleared again, but around noon on June 15 dark clouds were seen in the northeast and ash fell again for about an hour. [2]

The Native villages on Shelikof Strait, Douglas and Katmai, were naturally hit much more heavily by pumice than were villages to the north and upwind. In the morning of that first day — June 6 — explosions had been heard in the coastal villages, although no earth tremors were noticed, and many village people were able to flee down the coast. Those who were not, such as people fishing at Kaflia Bay, were evacuated from the pumice-laden shore some days later by a vessel sent from Kodiak.

With regard to the Severnovsk area, where ash piled up more than a foot deep, stories from survivors interviewed decades after the event indicated that when the massive eruption began a majority of the residents were already at the lower end of the Naknek River — possibly waiting for the opening of the fishing season and the canneries, possibly in partial response to the early earth tremors. According to one interview conducted in 1923, a man identified as Bob Scott had spent the night of June 5 at one of the Severnovsk villages, probably the larger Nunamiut settlement. June 5 had been clear, he said, giving no reason to expect anything unusual. But next day there were "great noises and earthquakes, which were almost continuous," and the air was filled with so much dust that it became dark. The Native people were in panic, he said, "and started down the lake in boats immediately, leaving many of their possessions behind. They kept close to the shore so as not to become lost" in the darkness. [3]

This is a far less dramatic account of the event than was related by Robert F. Griggs from an interview with American Pete that was conducted in 1918 by his assistant Paul Hagelbarger. American Pete, who was described by Griggs in his comprehensive report on the eruption as chief of the main Severnovsk village, was said to have had houses both at the Severnovsk settlement (Nunamiut) and "at Ukak, up the Valley," presumably closer to the Ukak River. "Warned by the earthquakes preliminary to the outburst," said Griggs from the interview, American Pete was at "Ukak" engaged in moving his belongings to "Savonoski," that is, to Nunamiut.

The Katmai Mountain blew up [American Pete is quoted as saying] with lots of fire, and fire came down trail from Katmai with lots of smoke. We go fast Savonoski [i.e., Nunamiut]. Everybody get in bidarka.... Helluva job. We come Naknek one day, dark, no could see. Hot ash fall. Work like hell... Never can go back to... libe [sic] again. Everything ash. Good place, too, you bet. Fine trees, lots moose, bear and deer. Lots of fish in front of barabara. No many mosquitoes. Fine church, fine house.

Figure 50 – The chapel at the village of Nunamiut as it stood in 1940. National Park Service photo by F.T. Been. Compare with Figure 34, a view of the same building 21 years earlier.

Figure 51 – Across the slumped roof of a sod-covered house on the river bank at the abandoned village of Nunamiut, 1953; the Savonoski River and its pumice plain are in the background. Photo by W.A. Davis, on file at the Museum of Natural and Cultural History, University of Oregon. Compare with Figure 42, the same or similar houses 31 years earlier.

Interviews in the 1960s indicated that a couple of families had tried to move back to Severnovsk after the eruption, but had found it intolerable. Nevertheless, American Pete in 1918 professed to return to the area briefly each fall to hunt.

Despite ash deposits in depths of 8 inches to more than a foot, the actual recovery of the region around Naknek Lake was rapid. Although the lesser vegetation was smothered, trees not only survived but with the lack of competition experienced several years of improved well-being, as shown by the fat growth rings for those years that can be seen in cross-sections of spruce logs. The Naknek drainage salmon spawning was demolished for 1912, yet the damage was short-lived, with spawning resumed in the next year. Indeed, the southern Bristol Bay salmon catch, which depended on fish from both the Naknek and Kvichak river systems, was undiminished in 1912 and subsequent years.

The future of fugitives from the Severnovsk villages wasn't that simple a matter, however. With an ancient history of hostilities between them and the downstream Aglurmiut, it is possible that there was some regional hesitation about how they might be resettled. In any event, in the fall of 1912 a meeting between Native leaders of Naknek and of the Severnovsk settlements, moderated by the Orthodox priest from Nushagak, resulted in agreement that the upper-drainage people should establish a new settlement on the south bank of the Naknek River about 6 miles upriver from Naknek village. This settlement of Savonoski (originally "Novo-Savonoski" in church documents) came into being, and ultimately a new chapel was built and once again consecrated to Mary, Our Lady of Kazan, as had been the chapel at Nunamiut, and the (same?) chapel at the earlier Ikkhagmiut. [4]

Families
Severnovsk Settlements –

It was sometime around 1856, apparently, that Vasiliy Itug'yuk and Mariya Nuyalkak, both of the major Severnovsk settlement, were wedded — he aged 24 or 25, she 17 — although the wedding was not sanctified by the church until 1857. Mariya's family had evidently been resident in a Severnovsk settlement since early in the century, but whether this was true of her husband's people is not clear from available Nushagak church documents, although he was characterized as "Aleut." As noted earlier, the nineteenth century had seen many exchanges of residents between the Severnovsk villages and those of the Pacific coast, Douglas and Katmai.

According to church records, the first child of the new couple, Pavel, was baptized in 1857, the year the marriage was sanctified, and thereafter the couple had at least seven other children, not all of whom survived. The youngest was baptized as Pelagiya (or Pelagia, in the spelling preferred by her own later family), who according to the Russian Church vital statistics records for 1881, when the birth was recorded, had been born in 1879. In her early childhood she had three older brothers and three sisters, the youngest of them Tatiana, born in 1873. [5]

The 1880s and '90s of Pelagia's youth was the period in which foreign travelers passing through Katmai Pass and along the course of the Naknek drainage system were increasingly American rather than Russian, with most of them stopping at the Severnovsk settlement known as Ikkhagmiut. And if it is true, as was mentioned in an earlier section, that the end of the 1890s saw boats plying Naknek Lake in order to transport gold seekers on their way to the diggings at Nome, an increase in the relative cosmopolitanism of the hitherto isolated Severnovsk villages was inevitable. The further opening of the Bristol Bay region in the same decade through the development of canneries and an attendant arrival on the Bay of permanent residents of Scandinavian and other European descent, must also have tended to promote mingling of the resident ethnic groups of Natives.

In 1897 Pelagia married Petr Kayagvak, reportedly a resident of Nushagak who had accompanied the Nushagak priest, Father Vladimir Modestov, to the Severnovsk settlements as one of his guides. The priest's characterization of Petr as "guide," as well as his marriage to a local girl three days after the party arrived, certainly seems to say that he had visited the inland village before that year.

Categorized by church documents as a Kusquqvagmiut, Petr had been born in Togiak in 1872; his father and mother, Feodor Kayagvak and Natal'ya Anagakhkak, had been married at a village written by the officiating priest as Akulyak (possibly the settlement Aklut on the Kuskokwim River), [6] some ten years earlier. For a time after Petr's birth the family lived in Kanakanak, across Nushagak Bay from Nushagak village, where in 1886 Feodor Kayagvak died. Sometime afterward the widow and her son moved to Nushagak itself, and in so doing Petr must have found an opportunity for schooling, as will be seen.

According to Father Modestov, in 1897 his party had arrived at Ikkhagmiut on January 30, after a storm-punctuated trip from Egegik. In his report he uttered what seem to have been customary complaints about "debauchery, illicit cohabitation, giving girls to husbands before marriage," etc., and then stated that on February 2 he had married three couples, one of which was Petr and Pelagia. After a prayer service on February 3, the priest said, he gave *instruction... for Orthodox Christian life to the new toyon [the designated village head, who in this case was Pavel Itug'yuk, Pelagia's oldest brother] and to my guide Petr Kayagvak, a Nushagak resident married the day before to a Severnovsk girl and newly appointed by me as reader in their chapel. I left him here with the goal of replacing the old reader, nearly entirely illiterate, and with the goal of teaching the children reading and writing, and the adults behavior.*

A year later Father Modestov felt that he could report little improvement in adult behavior, although "debauchery has decreased in comparison with the preceding year." But, on the other hand, *the young generation of the settlement residents this year gladdened me with success at school; in both settlements there were grammar schools this winter, where my guide Petr Kayagvak, left by me last year, made an effort at teaching. The male and female students read Russian and Slavonic rather well and have learned to write letters [of the alphabet].* [7]

A report of the following year, 1899, concerning Alaskan schools sponsored by the Russian Church, indicated that the major Severnovsk settlement had a primary school with 17 students, the teacher of whom was one P. Kayagvak. [8]

But there is some minor confusion regarding the continuity of residence at Ikkhagmiut of Petr Kayagvak and his wife. Late in 1897 the child Feodor had been born to them and baptized at Nushagak. And the Nushagak confessional register for that year listed not only Petr's widowed mother, but also Petr and his wife Pelagia as present at that place. In 1899 the Nushagak register again lists Petr and Pelagia as present there, although by this time Petr's mother has disappeared, presumably deceased; and yet surprisingly no child is listed for the young Kayagvaks. They do not appear in later Nushagak registers.

There is no confessional register for Ikkhagmiut in 1900, and although there was a federal census of the settlement taken that year, identifications are hampered both by the garbling of names and by the fact that even then the census taker entered only given names, without bothering to try to understand Native surnames. One pair may represent an attempt to list Petr and Pelagia, although no child for them is included. By 1904, however, when a confessional register for the Severnovsk settlement reappears, Petr, Pelagia, and their son Feodor are recorded together.

But confusion produced by church records does not end there.

In 1905 the priest visiting the village reported in the margin of the confessional register that Petr had died. There is, however, no confirming report in the church records of vital statistics, and later events make it rather evident that Petr was simply absent from Ikkhagmiut, where Pelagia evidently remained to be listed by the priest as a widow [9] although present evidence seems to indicate otherwise. Whereas Pelagia was shown again as a widow in the next available Ikkhagmiut confessional register, of 1909, the vital statistics records of 1910 list a second child, a daughter Elezaveta, born to her and to Petr Kayagvak on April 7, and baptized the same month. Once again, following the volcanic eruption of 1912 and the relocation of the Severnovsk settlements to the down-river Savonoski, the confessional register of 1913 lists Pelagia as a widow, now accompanied by her son Feodor (without Elezaveta), but for February of the same year the vital statistics record the birth of a daughter named Marina to Pelagia and Petr. Wherever he may have been in these periods, Petr Kayagvak was evidently far from dead.

By then, Petr had become "American Pete," the name he was commonly referred to, at least by non-Natives, in preference to the name that appears in the church records. And as American Pete he was immortalized as the closest Severnovsk witness to the eruption of Novarupta in 1912 when he was interviewed by Paul Hagelbarger of the Griggs volcano research team in 1918. Some local people believe he died that same year. In any event, Petr Kayagvak's vital state was clearly reversed by the following year, for it was then, in 1919, that the true widow Pelagia remarried. Her second husband, Nikolai Melgenak, by some accounts was also from the Severnovsk settlements, although a family tradition says that he was originally from Douglas on Shelikof Strait. Reportedly born in 1892, he was somewhat more than ten years Pelagia's junior.[10] Like Petr Kayagvak, he also acquired a nickname: after a hunting accident caused him to lose an arm, he became One Arm Nick. Despite this disability, however, local people credited him with much of the construction of the chapel in the new Savonoski settlement.

The Melgenaks would be important inhabitants of the new down-river settlement, but there were other families of note there as well.

Like the family of Pelagia's mother Mariya, the family of Andrei Anshaiknak (also known as Andrei Kanuya), who was born around 1850, had been resident in the Severnovsk area at least since early in the nineteenth century. Andrei and his wife Dariya had at least six children; youngest was Trifon, born around 1880. In 1905 Trifon married Ekaterina Shul'iak — the daughter of Pelagia's older sister Tatiana and her Kiatiirmiut husband Simeon Pan'ian, who had married in 1888. The second son of the marriage of Trifon and Ekaterina was a younger Trifon, often called Trofim or Trefim, later to spell his name Trefon. [11] Born in 1910, he was little more than a baby at the time of eruption.

Albatross-Alaska-1900
Bristol Bay Dist .

Native village and Ukala Rack
on bluff to W.ᵈ of Artic Packing Co. (
Naknek River

Figure 52 – The Native village of 1900 located west of the Arctic Packing Co. in what is today South Naknek. Fish and Wildlife photo no. 22-FFA-2542, U.S. National Archives.

Together with most of the Severnovsk people, the families of Pelagia and Trifon had moved to the new village Savonoski, which in their language they referred to as Ulutluq — a name that reportedly indicated a rising tide, or perhaps a tidally flooded place. In the 1913 confessional register for the new settlement Trifon was listed first, evidently recognized as toyon or village head. [12] Later, like many people of the new Savonoski village, Trifon would move farther downstream to the settlements nearer the mouth of the Naknek River. His son's family name was recorded as *Angasan* when the young Trefon entered school.

On the eve of the volcanic eruption the Severnovsk inhabitants had totaled slightly fewer than 100 people. Although most of them must have moved temporarily to the new, downriver village, within a few years most of them would, like Trifon, disperse among other settlements where they had relatives or particular interests. In 1918 the population of Savonoski was only a little more than 50. [13]

Naknek River Villages –

As indicated earlier, although there were a few births recorded for the Severnovsk settlements in which the ethnicity of the child (depending from that of the father) was indicated as Kusquqvagmiut or Kiatiirmiut, no births of children were identified as Aglurmiut until after 1880. The small number of these identified non-Alutiiq births prohibits any strong reliance on them as showing real differences in acceptance of outsiders from certain other Native ethnic groups, but

91

they do seem to suggest that the reduction of hostile feelings between Alutiit of Severnovsk and Aglurmiut of the lower Naknek River was somewhat slow in coming. The listings of births and marriages at Paugvik also record little close contact with their Alutiiq neighbors before the end of the nineteenth century.

At Paugvik the Chukan family appears in a number of entries in Russian Church documents of births and marriages in the nineteenth-century, revealing the family's presence there since early in the 1800s. It was about then, according to interviews conducted around Naknek, that the ancestors of Paul Chukan (born 1901 in Naknek) must have come to the area. By one account, his great-grandfather had told a descendant that his earlier family came "from the north;" according to another, Paul Chukan's great-great grandparents themselves had come from the vicinity of Nunivak Island. [14]

According to Russian Church vital statistics records, Paul Chukan's parents, Konstantin Chukan and Evdokiya Tuliman, were married in 1896. Konstantin himself had been born in Paugvik in 1872, to parents Nikita Chukan and Anna Panikhpigak. A record of the birth of Nikita couldn't be located, although given the sketchiness of recorded entries before the 1860s its absence isn't surprising. One would expect that Konstantin's great-grandfather would have been born a little earlier than AD 1800. In any event, this paternal family seems to have been representative of the Aglurmiut immigrants to the shores of Bristol Bay sometime around the beginning

of the nineteenth century. But Paul Chukan married Anna Andrews, then living at Levelock on the lower Kvichak River, whom members of the family believe to have been born at Douglas village in the area of Alutiiq speech.

The shift of the Severnovsk people to the lower reaches of the Naknek River was most certainly contributing to the reduction of any tension that had existed between upper and lower drainage people, as formerly unfriendly groups of people intermingled more and more. When the elder Trifon Anshaiknak's wife Ekaterina died, he remarried, this time to Paul Chukan's aunt, also named Ekaterina or Katherine. According to one story, when Paul Chukan's daughter Anisha was a baby she was frequently tucked below the deck of the elder Trifon's kayak and paddled around; according to numerous other reports Paul Chukan and the younger Trefon were often partners in trapping and other activities. [15]

Although it may well have been tempting for original Severnovsk people resettled in the lower-drainage village of Savonoski to return upriver as the region healed after the trauma of the eruption, in 1918 Katmai National Monument was created by declaration of President Wilson. As it was zoned from the beginning, before all later expansions, the Monument included the eastern half of Iliuk Arm and the lower Savonoski River — the area of the abandoned Severnovsk villages. Any return to the former home was thus effectively discouraged.

Influenza

The impact of the epidemic respiratory illnesses that ended the lives of so many Naknek drainage people in the nineteenth century had fallen most heavily on individuals in their active years — those from about ages 15 to 60 — rather than upon the very young and the very old. On a more nearly worldwide basis, this same pattern of adult mortality characterized the influenza pandemic of 1918-1919.[16]

This great epidemic, which reportedly took more than twenty million lives throughout the world, missed Bristol Bay in its first year, but arrived with a vengeance in its second. By some reports the disease entered the area with Asian cannery laborers, by another it was brought in by an Orthodox priest who held services that spring at Nushagak. Although neither is verified, the latter appears the more likely, given the appearance of the disease before the major crews of cannery workers arrived. The first Alaska Packers Association (APA) vessels had entered Bristol Bay and anchored in Nushagak Bay on May 19, to discover a winterman at the Clark's Point cannery and Natives in the nearby village already sick with influenza.

Across Bristol Bay, the first APA ship anchored off the Naknek River on May 22, and it was on May 26 that the first influenza cases were identified by the cannery physician, Dr. Frederick Spencer, when three Native men reported to the cannery hospital for help. Thus recognized, the Native settlement that had grown up near the (South) Naknek APA cannery was placed immediately under quarantine, and all cannery workers forbidden to go near it. On the following day, 38 people, all local Natives, were found to be suffering from the flu, and the numbers continued to grow; the first two deaths occurred by June 1. By that time the entire Native population near the cannery was infected. A gang of cannery workers was selected to help the physician and his nurses distribute daily food and medicines to the sick.

Meanwhile, the APA cannery superintendent from Naknek had visited the cannery at Ugashik, which was under his control, only to find that the disease had spread through the coastal village there, with one Native man dead. Six non-Native wintermen were also sick. On June 4, twelve Native deaths were reported. That day the Naknek APA cannery wired the Coast Guard Cutter *Unalga* requesting help for Ugashik.

On June 5 Dr. Spencer visited Savonoski village to find virtually everyone sick. The following day a party returned to the village with food and other supplies, and buried twelve dead. In the absence of coffins, bodies were wrapped separately in canvas for burial. Another person was buried there on June 8, and on that same day the APA superintendent radioed the United States Commissioner in Dillingham that about 80 people were known dead in the Naknek vicinity, with an additional 21 at Ugashik. Shortly thereafter, nearly all remaining Savonoski people were transferred to the vicinity of the APA cannery, where two

Albatross -Alaska-1900
Bristol Bay Dist.

Canning Plant of Artic Packing Co. (A. P. A.) Naknek River. general view from bluff to S.? Showing headlands at entrance.

Figure 53 – View in 1900 of the plant of the Arctic Packing Co, Alaska Packers Association, now South Naknek. It was here that influenza-infected Native people were cared for during the 1919 epidemic. Fish and Wildlife photo no. 22-FFA-2539, U.S. National Archives.

large tents were erected on wooden platforms and equipped with bedding to serve as a hospital. On June 9, a temporary orphanage was prepared at the APA cannery in an old hospital building. Nineteen orphans were provided clean clothes, daily hot food, and medical attention under the charge of a special nurse.

Somewhat later, June 19, a small amount of medicine was received at Naknek from the U.S. Navy ship *Marblehead*, and at about the same time the *U.S.S. Vicksburg* arrived off Ugashik to remain for a couple of weeks, burying dead in the coastal village (now Pilot Point), and providing some medical assistance to the upper village (present Ugashik), where the disease had spread. In early July a special shipment of medicines, fresh vegetables, and other provisions was received in Bristol Bay from APA headquarters in Seattle. By mid-July the major sickness was ameliorating at both Naknek and Ugashik, never having seriously struck the village at Egegik.

A problem remaining was the disposition of the large number of children who were orphaned by the epidemic. That summer, following directions from the Coast Guard, an APA vessel transported 32 orphans from Naknek and Ugashik across Bristol Bay to the government hospital in Dillingham. According to a report on the situation by the APA superintendent at Naknek, the surviving Native adults there were furnished during their convalescence with both food and medical attention, and were given light jobs during the following winter (painting boats, etc.) in order to allow them to be self-supporting.

A total of about 90 Native people had been cared for in the temporary hospital near the APA cannery. The final tally of the dead buried by cannery crews, according to the APA superintendent, was about 40 from the coastal Ugashik village, 52 who died in the vicinity of the Naknek cannery, and thirteen at Savonoski. There were apparently others who had been assisted in their sickness by the cannery on the north side of the river at Naknek proper. [17]

The severity of the impact of the epidemic on the Native community in the Naknek region is almost inconceivable to those of us who have grown up surrounded by developed twentieth-century medicine. The 65 people dying on the south shore of the Naknek River amounted to around half of the adult Native population. At (north) Naknek the parents of young Paul Chukan were among those who died, and although he was himself sick, he survived. On the other hand, one report is that there was no sickness in the home of Pelagia and her husband Nikolai Melgenak in Savonoski, because Pelagia insisted that the door be kept closed and no one admitted while the sickness raged. [18] The single enumeration sheet for Savonoski in the federal census of 1920 lists only 22 residents.

Notes

[1] The situation of 1900 with regard to commercial fishing is drawn from Moser (1902), that of 1905 from U.S. House of Representatives (1906). Naknek-Kvichak catchment sizes are recorded in ADF&G (1973). Summer practices of much of the Native population were described in local interviews conducted principally in the 1960s and 1970s.

[2] The general course of the eruption is covered by Griggs (1922), but the account is considerably refined by Hildreth and Fierstein (2000). The logs of vessels of the Alaska Packers Association, anchored in Larsen Bay and Bristol Bay during the eruption and all describing the ash fall, were consulted in the Maritime Museum, San Francisco. With the addition of this information regarding Naknek, the course of the eruption appears to be somewhat extended (i.e., from June 6 to June 12, with more ash on June 15) from the account provided by Hildreth and Fierstein, who on the basis of information especially from Kodiak describe the major eruptive action as lasting only about 60 hours beginning on June 6. A more general summary of volcanism in the immediate area, as well as additional information regarding geology, is to be found in Riehle (2002).

[3] Quoted from Fenner (1925:216). Later interviews referred to were those conducted at the village of Savonoski on the lower Naknek River, with Mrs. Pelagia Melgenak and others unidentified in 1953, and with both Mrs. Melgenak and Mike McCarlo in 1961 (Davis 1954:68-71; 1961).

[4] Details in this section are drawn from interviews conducted in the 1970s, and with reference also to Black (1984). Fish data are from internal reports of the Alaska Department of Fish and Game. The question of the relationship of Ikkhagmiut to Nunamiut is raised in the preceding chapter.

[5] Alaska Russian Church (1733-1938, Nushagak confessional registers), (1816 - 1936, Nushagak vital statistics). In the confessional register for 1881 she is listed as age 1.

[6] Although the Native name for Naknek Lake was reported by Vasil'ev to be Akulogak (superficially similar to Akulyak), the fact that both of Petr's parents were classed as Kusquqwagmiut suggests that the Kuskokwim village is the more likely interpretation. See appropriate entries in Baker (1901).

[7] Alaska Russian Church (1733-1938), Nushagak church service registers, January 1 - December 31, 1897, and January 1 - December 31, 1898 (Vladimir Modestov). Translations are by Katherine Arndt, to whom I am grateful for references.

[8] Antonius (1899:158-159, 163). Again, I thank Katherine Arndt for this reference.

[9] The 1905 confessional register (Alaska Russian Church 1733-1938, Nushagak) is evidently a copy of the 1904 register, in which by marginal notations the priest brought it up to date from his apparent 1905 visit. It is among these notations that the entry "died" appears. In the next clear register, of 1909, Pelagia is listed as a widow, although a somewhat garbled entry in the federal census of 1910 probably represents the couple at the village at that time designated Nunamiut. An account by one local man, now deceased, asserted that Petr Kayagvak acquired the nickname by which he was known later – American Pete – as the result of a sojourn in San Francisco. It is possible that an extended trip to the south was responsible for his absence in 1905 and perhaps later years.

[10] The 1920 federal census enumeration sheet actually lists her as 39, him as 30 — ages that do not precisely match the available vital records.

[11] Here for convenience I use the spelling Trifon for the father, Trefon for the son.

12 The vernacular name of the village is published by Feldman (2001), who obtained it in interviews; it also appears on the 1929 confessional register of Savonoski (Alaska Russian Church 1733-1938, Nushagak), as was pointed out to me by Katherine Arndt. Trifon in the 1913 confessional register is listed as Trifon Kanuya, the latter being the alternative name by which a number of the family members had appeared in various registers.

13 The genealogical details are derived from examinations of Russian church documents of the Nushagak parish, with a special debt to Katherine Arndt for sharing the results of her unpublished research into related Russian documents, and to Kerry Feldman for copies of two separate contract research reports dealing with the Naknek region. Some family details are drawn from Black (1984), who also reports her conclusion from church documents that Petr Kayakvak died around 1905. Nevertheless, the local tradition that Petr Kayagvak and American Pete were the same person is strong enough to indicate that a mistake was made by the church recorders, and that Petr was alive through most of the second decade of the twentieth century. References to the volcanic eruption involve matter in Griggs (1922); size of the Savonoski population in 1918 is from Davis (1954:71).

14 For the first account I am indebted to Kerry Feldman's citation of his interviews in the 1970s, for the second I draw on my own interviews with Paul Chukan's daughter in the same decade, when she also made it clear that her parents were speakers of a variant of Central Yupik as against the Alutiiq spoken by people of Savonoski, Ugashik, and Kodiak.

15 In addition to material from Alaska Russian Church (1816-1936, Nushagak), this section draws heavily on draft material provided by Kerry Feldman from his work in the King Salmon and Naknek area in very recent years.

16 The effect in the Naknek region in the nineteenth century, as reported earlier, is documented in Dumond (1986, especially Figure 8). With regard to the mortality pattern in the pandemic of 1918-19, see Burnet and White (1972:202-205).

17 The U.S. National Archives, Records Group 126, Office of Territories Classified Files, 1907-1951, Box 468, 9-1-71, "Alaska, Health Conditions," contains (a) reports of APA superintendents and physicians for Naknek, Nushagak, and Kvichak regarding the epidemic, all of which were transmitted by the president of APA to the Secretary of the Interior on Oct. 27, 1919; and (b) report of the 1919 Alaska cruise of the USCGC Unalga , transmitted by the Secretary of the Treasury to the Secretary of the Interior on Jan. 28, 1920. The present account relies principally on the included reports of J. F. Heinbockel, superintendent, and Frederick B. Spencer, medical officer, of the APA Naknek Station.

18 These are based on interviews.

Into the Twentieth

Events of the late nineteenth century and the first two decades of the twentieth set the stage for events that came later and with ever increasing speed. But they scarcely forecast the complexities of the new century as it unfolded. Outside influences here would again drastically modify the local world, a world that had seen its share of changes in the millennia of its history.

With the introduction of the commercial fishing industry came the arrival of European fishermen, predominently Scandinavian. Some of them were seasonal, but others married into local communities around Bristol Bay and left their unmistakable mark on later censuses by means of hitherto foreign names. In the census of 1900, taken in wintertime, there were already six such men living in the villages near the mouth of the Naknek River.

As market fishing expanded, so did this immigrant portion of the population, and with the loss of virtually half of the Natives in the influenza epidemic of 1919, the total count of Natives sank rapidly below that of the newcomers. By 1920 there were more than a dozen canneries located on both sides of the lower Naknek River and along the east bank of Bristol Bay northward to the lower Kvichak River. Providing jobs, and shipping in building and other materials, these industrial establishments both drove and controlled the local economy, although changes in the early 1930s did permit fishing from the beach with set gillnets — an occupation with relatively low requirements for capital that allowed local residents, including many Natives, to fish more

independently. A few others of the local people, together with immigrants from Norwegian Lapland, were involved in a relatively short-lived reindeer industry that lasted through the 1930s but ended in the 1940s, when remnant herds were abandoned to run with the native caribou.

In 1905 the first Naknek post office had been established, featuring monthly mail delivery in summer by ship, in winter by dogsled that connected with ships at Kanatak, located on what is now Portage Bay on the Pacific coast across the Alaska Peninsula. Mail delivery directly to the south side of the lower Naknek River was slower; the South Naknek post office was established only in 1937. By the early 1920s there was a public grade school in Naknek that serviced children from both sides of the river. Again, a school in South Naknek came later, being established in the 1950s. [1]

In the years after 1912 the volcanic-ash-covered region of the Naknek lake system recovered rapidly. In the 1920s trappers claimed cabins around the lake and its tributaries; these included some area Natives, but even more immigrants from outside. When the boundary of Katmai National Monument was shifted westward in 1931, incorporating all but the western end of Naknek Lake, trapping for most of these pioneer entrepreneurs was rendered illegal under U.S. law. Nevertheless, with no surveillance by the National Park Service in the early years of the Monument, there was no enforcement. This circumstance began to change only after 1938, when notice of the situation by the Alaska Game

Figure 54 to the left – Pelagia Melgenak at her home in Savonoski in 1961. Photo by W.A. Davis, on file at the Museum of Natural and Cultural History, University of Oregon.

99

Commission brought an investigation that resulted in a few arrests, and all but a very few of the trappers vacated the area. [2] A formal National Park Service presence in the Monument would begin in the 1950s.

World War II saw the construction of the U.S. military air base at King Salmon, the beginning of really close communication between the Naknek area communities and major cities of the world. The war also carried some young men away to war in far-off places. And its aftermath brought further immigration, heightened commerce, a variety of new government installations, and increased employment opportunities for local people. With the inevitable expansion in these cosmopolitan ties, there came by the early 1960s increasing Native consciousness of rights to territory and the first steps toward creation of Native councils. By now the sense of ethnic distinctions between Native groups of different histories was rapidly being lost in return for a growing feeling of Native unity to stand in the face of outside forces.

At the end of the decade of the '60s, the Alaska Native Claims Settlement Act finally provided a legal basis for the recognition of Native rights and actual control of lands. Yet concurrent with this was a formalization of the ownership or control of other lands by the State of Alaska and by Federal agencies such as the U.S. Fish and Wildlife Service, the Bureau of Land Management, and the National Park Service. As a part of this, Katmai National Monument was again expanded, and this time designated Katmai National Park and Preserve. It now enveloped all of the upper Naknek drainage system, hence asserting further limits on activities in much of the region.

And so rests the story to be told here — a story not ended, but changed. Changed radically in detail as the forces of the entire world have come to impinge on a small and once isolated region, come with its amazing resources of technology and communication as they impinge in the same way on all small regions everywhere. Radical changes in details, but perhaps not so much in essence.

For in the 10,000 years of its known history the Naknek region has repeatedly withstood thrusts from the world outside, as well as cataclysms from its own mountains of fire. These have included the arrival of the first human hunters; the volcanic eruption of 2000 BC; the arrival of tlhe first river fishermen of the Gomer period with what was surely a revolutionary outlook; the eruption of 1000 BC; the arrival and development of the fishing people of the Brooks River period; the incursion from the north by people of the Brooks River Camp phase; the volcanic eruption of AD 1350; the reoccupation of the northern Alaska Peninsula by people from the direction of Kodiak to form the Brooks River Bluffs phase; the concurrent AD 1800 invasions of Aglurmiut and Russians that is indicated by the Pavik phase; the sale to America and the increasing presence of Euro-Americans in the late nineteenth century; and the eruption of 1912.

The aftermath is still developing. So here the story must rest for now, although it surely does not end.

Notes

1 For much of this brief summary I am indebted to the historical sketch of Morris (1994), focused especially on South Naknek.

2 The trapping interlude is described in Clemens and Norris (1999:Chapt. 8).

The King Salmon River on the Alaska Peninsula, photo by M. Woodbridge Williams, 1973.

Ackerman, Robert E., and Lillian Ackerman
1973   Ethnoarchaeological Interpretations of Territoriality and Land Use in Southwestern Alaska. *Ethnohistory* 20: 315-334.

ADF&G (Alaska Department of Fish and Game)
1973   Bristol Bay Stock Status Report.   Unpublished document compiled by Steve Pennoyer, on file at ADF&G, Division of Commercial Fisheries, Anchorage.

Alaska Russian Church
1816-   Archives, Series E (Vital Statistics). Records of the Russian Orthodox Greek
1936   Catholic Church of North America, Diocese of Alaska. Library of Congress Manuscript Division, shelf no. 12,766.
1733-   Archives, Series D (Geographic File). Records of the Russian Orthodox Greek
1938   Catholic Church of North America, Diocese of Alaska. Library of Congress Manuscript Division, shelf no. 19,001.

Anderson, Douglas D.
1988   Onion Portage: The Archaeology of a Stratified Site from the Kobuk River, Northwest Alaska. *Anthropological Papers of the University of Alaska* 22(1-2).

Antonius, Hieromonk
1899   Report on the School Work of the Russian Orthodox Church in Alaska.   Russian *American Orthodox Messenger* 4(8):155-163.

Baker, Marcus
1901   Geographic Dictionary of Alaska. *Bulletin of the United States Geological Survey* 187. Washington: Government Printing Office.

Beach, Rex
1909   *The Silver Horde*. New York: Harper and Brothers.
1940   *Personal Exposures*. New York: Harper and Brothers.

Bever, Michael R., and Michael L. Kunz, eds.
2001   Between Two Worlds: Late Pleistocene Cultural and Technological Diversity in Eastern Beringia. *Arctic Anthropology* 38(2).

Bixby, William
1965   *Track of the Bear*. New York: David McKay.

Black, Lydia T.
1984   Letter to J. W. Tanner, National Park Service, July 31. On file at the Alaska Regional Office, National Park Service.

Bland, Richard L., P. L. McClenahan, and D. E. Dumond
1998   Archeological Report on Excavations Conducted in 1994 at XMK-008, Brooks River National Historic Landmark, Katmai National Park and Preserve, Alaska. Manuscript report, Cultural Resource Division, National Park Service Alaska System Support Office, Anchorage.

Bundy, Barbara E., Dale M. Vinson, and Don E. Dumond
2005   Brooks River Cutbank: An Archeological Data Recovery Project of the National Park Service in Katmai National Park, Alaska. *University of Oregon Anthropological Papers* 64.

Burnet, Sir Macfarlane, and David O. White
1972   *Natural History of Infectious Disease* (4th ed.). Cambridge: Cambridge University Press.

Clark, Donald W.
1984   Pacific Eskimo: Historical Ethnography. In "Arctic," D. Damas, ed., pp. 185-197. *Handbook of North American Indians* 5, W. T. Sturtevant, gen ed. Washington, DC: Smithsonian Institution.

Clark, Gerald H.
1977   Archaeology on the Alaska Peninsula: The Coast of Shelikof Strait, 1963-1965. *University of Oregon Anthropological Papers* 13.

Clemens, Janet, and Frank Norris
1999   *Building in an Ashen Land: Katmai National Park and Preserve Historic Resource Study*. Anchorage: National Park Service Alaska Support Office.

Collins, Henry B.
1964   The Arctic and Subarctic. In *Prehistoric Man in the New World*, J. D. Jennings and E. Norbeck, eds., pp. 85-114. Chicago: University of Chicago Press.

Davis, Wilbur A.
1954   Archaeological Investigations of Inland and Coastal Sites of the Katmai National Monument, Alaska. Report to the U.S. National Park Service. Department of Anthropology, University of Oregon, Eugene. [Also as *Archives of Archaeology* No. 4. University of Wisconsin Press, Microfiche.]
1961   Mount Katmai Eruption. Transcript of a tape recording made in July-August (typescript), submitted with "Report to National Park Service, Region Four, on Tape Recordings of Eyewitness Accounts of Mt. Katmai Eruption of June 6, 1912," by L. S. Cressman. University of Oregon, January 1962.

Detterman, Robert L.
1986   Glaciation of the Alaska Peninsula. In *Glaciation in Alaska: The Geologic Record*, T. D. Hamilton, K. M. Reed, and R. M. Thorson, eds., pp. 151-170. Anchorage: Alaska Geological Society.

Dikov, N. N., and E. E. Titov
1984   Problems of the Stratification and Periodization of the Ushki Sites. *Arctic Anthropology* 21(2):69-80.

Dumond, Don E.
1962   Prehistory in the Naknek Drainage: A Preliminary Statement. In "Research on Northwest Prehistory: Prehistory in the Naknek Drainage, Southwestern Alaska," by L. S. Cressman and D. E. Dumond. Final Report to the National Science Foundation, August 31, 1962. Department of Anthropology, University of Oregon.
1977   *The Eskimos and Aleuts*. London: Thames and Hudson.
1981   Archaeology on the Alaska Peninsula: The Naknek Region, 1960-1975. *University of Oregon Anthropological Papers* 21.
1986   Demographic Effects of European Expansion: A Nineteenth-Century Native Population on the Alaska Peninsula. *University of Oregon Anthropological Papers* 35.
1988   Trends and Traditions in Alaskan Prehistory: A New Look at an Old View of the Neo-Eskimo. In "The Late Prehistoric Development of Alaska's Native People," R. D. Shaw, R.K. Harritt, and D. E. Dumond, eds., pp. 17-26. *Aurora: Alaska Anthropological Association* Monograph Series 4.

1994   A Reevaluation of Late Prehistoric Houses of the Naknek River Region, Southwestern Alaska. *Arctic Anthropology* 31(2):108-118.

2000   The Norton Tradition. *Arctic Anthropology* 37(2):1-22.

2003   The Leader Creek Site and Its Context. *University of Oregon Anthropological Papers* 60.

Dumond, Don E., and James W. VanStone
1995   Paugvik: A Nineteenth-Century Native Village on Bristol Bay, Alaska. *Fieldiana Anthropology* (n.s.) 24. Chicago: Field Museum of Natural History.

Elliott, Henry W.
1886   *Our Arctic Province: Alaska and the Seal Islands.* New York: Charles Scribner's Sons.

Erickson, Jared
2003   Appendix C: The Geoarchaeology of Multiroom Houses at 49-NAK-8. In "The Leader Creek Site and Its Context," by D. E. Dumond, pp. 141-164. *University of Oregon Anthropological Papers* 60.

Fedorova, Svetlana G.
1973   The Russian Population in Alaska and California: Late 18th Century — 1867. Kingston, Ontario: Limestone Press.

Feldman, Kerry D.
2001   Ethnohistory and the IRA Tribal Status Application of King Salmon Natives, Alaska. *Alaska Journal of Anthropology* 1(1):100-117.

Fenner, Clarence N.
1925   Earth Movements Accompanying the Katmai Eruption. *Journal of Geology* 33:116-139, 193-223.

Fienup-Riordan, Ann
1990   Yup'ik Warfare and the Myth of the Peaceful Eskimo. In Eskimo Essays: *Yup'ik Lives and How We See Them*, pp. 146-166. New Brunswick: Rutgers University Press.

Finney, Bruce P., I. Gregory-Evans, M. S. V. Douglas, and J. P. Smol
2002   Fisheries Productivity in the Northeastern Pacific Ocean over the Past 2,200 Years. *Nature* 416:729-733.

Giddings, James Louis
1964   *The Archaeology of Cape Denbigh.* Providence: Brown University Press.

Giddings, J. L., and Douglas D. Anderson
1986   Eskimo and Pre-Eskimo Settlements around Kotzebue Sound, Alaska. *National Park Service Publications in Archaeology* No. 20. Washington: U.S. Department of the Interior.

Goebel, Ted, Michael R. Waters, and Margarita Dikova.
2003   The Archaeology of Ushki Lake, Kamchatka, and the Pleistocene Peopling of the Americas. *Science* 301(5632):501-505.

Griggs, Robert F.
1922   *The Valley of Ten Thousand Smokes.* Washington, D.C.: The National Geographic Society.

Guthrie, R. Dale
2004   Radiocarbon evidence of mid-Holocene mammoths stranded on an Alaskan Bering Sea island. *Nature* 429:746-749.

Harritt, Roger K.
1988   The Late Prehistory of Brooks River, Alaska. *University of Oregon Anthropological Papers* 38.
1994   Eskimo Prehistory on the Seward Peninsula, Alaska. Resource Report NPS/ARORCR/CRR-93/21. Anchorage: National Park Service, Alaska Region.
1997   Problems in Protohistoric Ethnogenesis in Alaska: The Naknek Drainage and the Pacific Eskimo Area. *Arctic Anthropology* 34(2):45-73.

Henn, Winfield
1978   Archaeology on the Alaska Peninsula: The Ugashik Drainage. 1973-1975. *University of Oregon Anthropological Papers* 14.

Hildreth, Wes, and Judy Fierstein
2000   Katmai Volcanic Cluster and the Great Eruption of 1912. GSA Bulletin 112(10):1594-1620.

Hilton, Michael R.
2002   Results of the 2001 Interior Rivers Survey: Reconnaissance-Level Pedestrian Survey of Alagnak and Savonoski River Corridors, Katmai National Park and Preserve, Alaska. Report of the NPS Cultural Resources Program on file at Lake Clark Katmai Studies Center. Anchorage.

Holmes, Charles E., and J. David McMahan
1996   1994 Archaeological Investigations at the Igiugig Airport Site (ILI-002). *Alaska Department of Natural Resources, Office of History and Archaeology Report* 57.

Hussey, John A.
1971   Embattled Katmai: A History of Katmai National Monument. Bound, typescript report of the Office of History and Historic Architecture, Western Service Center, National Park Service. San Francisco.

Kaufman, D.S. and C.H. Thompson
1998   Re-evaluation of pre-late Winsconsin glacial deposits, Lower Naknek River Valley, Southwestern Alaska, USA. *Arctic and Alpine Research* 30. No 2.142-153.

Knecht, Richard A.
1995   The Late Prehistory of the Alutiiq People: Culture Change on the Kodiak Archipelago from 1200-1750 A.D. Ph.D. dissertation in anthropology, Bryn Mawr College. Bryn Mawr, Pa.

Knecht, Richard A., and Richard H. Jordan
1985   Nunakakhnak: A Historic Koniag Village in Karluk, Kodiak Island, Alaska. *Arctic Anthropology* 22(2)L17-35.

Krauss, Michael
1982   Native Peoples and Languages of Alaska (map). Alaska Native Language Center, University of Alaska, Fairbanks.

Krech, Shepard III
1989   *A Victorian Earl in the Arctic.* Seattle: University of Washington Press.

Larsen, Helge
1950   Archaeological Investigations in Southwestern Alaska. *American Antiquity* 15(3):177-186.

Larsen, Helge, and Froelich Rainey
    1948   Ipiutak and the Arctic Whale Hunting Culture. *Anthropological Papers of the American Museum of Natural History* 42.

Leer, Jeff
    1991   Evidence for a Northern Northwest Coast Language Area: Promiscuous Number Marking and Periphrastic Possessive Constructions in Haida, Eyak, and Aleut. *IJAL* 37(2):158-193.
Lütke, Frederic
    1836   *Voyage atour de monde execute par ordre de La Magesté l'Empereur Nicolas 1er, sur la corvette* Le Séniavine *dans les annés 1826, 1827, 1828 et 1829*, J. Boyue trans. *Parte nautique.* St. Petersburg: C. Hintze.

MacNeish, Richard S.
    1956   The Engigstciak Site on the Yukon Arctic Coast. *Anthropological Papers of the University of Alaska* 4(2):91-104.

Mann, Daniel H., and Dorothy M. Peteet
    1994   Extent and Timing of the Last Glacial Maximum in Southwestern Alaska. *Quaternary Research* 42:136-148.

Morris, Judith M.
    1994   Katmai Research Project. Draft Technical Memorandum No. 2, Revised Draft Community Histories: Igiugig, Kokhanok, Levelock and South Naknek. Report by the National Resource and Environmental Policy Program and Department of Forest Resources, Utah State University, for the National Park Service Subsistence Division, Anchorage.

Moser, Jefferson F.
    1902   *The Salmon and Salmon Fisheries of Alaska: Report of the Alaskan Salmon Investigations of the United States Fish Commission Steamer Albatross in 1900 and 1901.* Washington: Government Printing Office.

Muller, Ernest H.
    1952   The Glacial Geology of the Naknek District, Bristol Bay Region, Alaska. Ph.D. dissertation, University of Illinois. Urbana, Ill.

Nowak, Michael
    1982   The Norton Period on Nunivak Island: Internal Change and External Influence. *Arctic Anthropology* 19(2):75-91.

O'Leary, Matthew
    1998   Preliminary Mitigation Report on NAK-015, Naknek River, Southwest Alaska. Report submitted to BIA [Bureau of Indian Affairs] Area Archaeology, Anchorage.

Petroff, Ivan
    1884   *Report on the Population, Industries, and Resources of Alaska.* Washington, DC: U.S. Government Printing Office.

Pierce, Richard A.
    1968   New Light on Ivan Petroff, Historian of Alaska. *Pacific Northwest Quarterly* 59(1):1-10.

Pitulko, V. V., P. A. Nikolsky, E. Yu. Girya, A. E. Basilyan, V. E. Tumskoy, S. A., Koulakov, S. N. Astakhov, E. Yu. Pavlova, and M. A. Anisimov
  2004   The Yana RHS Site: Humans in the Arctic Before the Last Glacial Maximum. *Science* 303:52-56.

Porter, R. P., compiler
  1893   *Report on the Population and Resources of Alaska at the 11th Census*: 1890. Washington, DC: Department of the Interior, Census Office.

Riehle, Jim
  2002   *The Geology of Katmai National Park and Preserve, Alaska*. Anchorage: Publication Consultants.

Riehle, James R., D. E. Dumond, C. E. Meyer, and J. M. Schaaf
  2000   Tephrochronology of the Brooks River Archaeology District, Katmai National Park and Preserve, Alaska. In "The Archaeology of Geological Catastrophes," W. J. McGuire, D. R. Griffiths, P. L. Hancock, and I. L. Steward, eds, pp. 245-266. *Geological Society Special Publication* 171. London.

Schaaf, Jeanne M.
  2004   *Witness: Firsthand Accounts of the Largest Volcanic Eruption in the Twentieth Century*. Anchorage: National Park Service.

Shaw, Robert D., and Charles E. Holmes, eds.
  1982   The Norton Interaction Sphere: Selected Papers from a Symposium. *Arctic Anthropology* 19(2).

Smith, Timothy A.
  1990   Compliance Testing Reveals Two Early Norton (Smelt Creek Phase) Occupations at Brooks River, Katmai National Park and Preserve. Paper presented at the annual meeting of the Alaska Anthropological Association, Fairbanks.

Solovjova, Katerina G., and Aleksandra A. Vovnyanko
  2002   *The Fur Rush*. Anchorage: Phenix Press.

Spurr, Josiah Edward
  1900   A Reconnaissance in Southwestern Alaska in 1898. "Twentieth Annual Report of the United States Geological Survey, Part VII," pp. 31-264. In *Annual Reports of the Department of the Interior for the Fiscal Year Ended June 30, 1899*. Washington: Government Printing Office.
  1950   The Log of the Kuskokwim: An Exploration in Alaska. Typescript compiled by Stephen H. Spurr. Rasmussen Library, University of Alaska Fairbanks.

Spurr, Josiah Edward, and W. S. Post
  1898   Explorations in Alaska, 1898. Map 3, Headwaters of Skwentna and Kuskokwim Rivers and Vicinity of Katmai. Map 4, Middle Kuskokwim River and Part of Bristol Bay. *In* Report, Public Resolution No. 25, 55th Congress, 3d Session.

Stillwell, K.B. and D.S. Kaufman
  1996   Late Winsconsin glacial history of the northern Alaska Peninsula, Southwestern Alska, USA. *Arctic and Alpine Research* 28. No 4.475-487.

Tikhmenev, Pavel A.
  1863   *Istoricheskoe obozrenie obrazovaniia Rossisko-Amerikanskoi kompanii i deistvie eio do nastoiashchego vremeni [A Historical Review of the Establishment of the Russian-American Company and Its Activity up to the Present Time]*, vol. 2. St. Petersburg.

Tilton, George Fred
  1928   *"Cap'n George Fred" Himself.* Garden City, N.Y: Doubleday, Doran.

U.S. House of Representatives
  1906   Protection and Regulation of the Fisheries of Alaska. Report 2657, 59th Congress, 1st Session. Washington, DC: Government Printing Office.

VanStone, James W.
  1967   *Eskimos of the Nushagak River: An Ethnographic History.* Seattle: University of Washington Press.
  1988   Russian Exploration in Southwestern Alaska: The Travel Journals of Petr Korsakovskiy (1818) and Ivan Ya. Vasilev (1829). Introduction by J.W. VanStone, trans. by D.H. Kraus. *Rasmuson Library Historical Translation Series* 4. Fairbanks: University of Alaska Press.

Woodbury, Anthony C.
1984   Eskimo and Aleut Languages. In "Arctic," D. Damas, ed., pp. 49-63. *Handbook of North American Indians* 5, W. T. Sturtevant, gen ed. Washington, DC: Smithsonian Institution.

Workman, William B., and Peter Zollars
  2002   The Dispersal of the Arctic Small Tool Tradition into Southern Alaska: Dates and Data from the Kenai Peninsula, Southcentral Alaska. *Anthropological Papers of the University of Alaska* (n.s.) 2(1):39-49.

Wrangell, F. P. von
  1980   Russian America: Statistical and Ethnographic Information, trans. by M. Sadouski. Kingston, Ontario: Limestone Press. [First publication, St. Petersburg, 1839.]

Afterword:

Figure 55 – From left to right Katherine Nudlash, Katie Trefon Hill, daughter Shirley Hill, and Billy Hill holding Frank Hill at the Libbyville cannery circa 1940 (photo courtesy of Shirley Hill Nielsen).

About five years ago Frank Hill suggested that the National Park Service produce a book on the cultural history of the people of the Naknek River. Mr. Hill reasoned such a book would be a good means to educate local students and the thousands of Katmai National Park and Preserve visitors that flock to the region each year about the history of the region. As a long time educator from the area Mr. Hill knew of what he spoke because the river originated in the park and a considerable amount of archeological, ethnographical and historical research had already been sponsored by the NPS.

Mr. Hill also has expert knowledge of the Naknek River. He was born at Iliamna village in 1939 when it was called Seversen's Roadhouse. His father, Billy Hill (1893-1946), a Finnish-born fisherman and shipwright, immigrated to the Bristol Bay along with thousands of other northern Europeans as a result of the salmon fishing industry starting in the late nineteenth and early twentieth centuries. Mr. Hill's mother was Katie Trefon, (1919-1994) a Lake Clark Dena'ina, who was born at Tanalian Point in 1919.

Mr. Hill and his siblings are thus like many Bristol Bay families, products of a fusion of European and Native Alaskan cultures that resulted when the hundreds of Euroamerican fishermen put down roots around the Bay by marrying Yup'ik, Alutiiq, or Dena'ina women. These unions created some of the leading families in the region. A small portion of the other prominent Bristol Bay Native families who can trace their ancestry from marriages similar to those of Billy and Katie Hill include: the Monsens, Aspelunds, Johnsons, Andersons, Nielsens, Petersons, and Holstroms from the Naknek River; the Roehls, Seversens, Herrmanns, Olsens, Hedlunds, and O'Neills from the Kvichak River; and the Bartmans, Olsons, Larsons, Schroeders, Hurleys, Nelsons, Samuelsons, Shades, Gardiners, and Krauses from the Nushagak River.

Mr. Hill was educated in public schools in Newhalen, Naknek, and Levelock before graduating from Wasilla High School in 1960. He spent two years in the U.S. Army (1963-1965), and was married to Dottie Baltzo in 1967 while they were both students at the University of Alaska Fairbanks; they graduated in 1969. Mr. Hill then taught high school mathematics and science in Anchorage until 1972, when he returned to Naknek to teach until 1977. Spending 1977 and 1978 studying at Cambridge, Massachusetts, where he was accompanied by his wife and their two young daughters Deirdre and Chamille, he received his master's degree in school administration and curriculum from Harvard Graduate School of Education. In 1984 and 1985 he did further graduate work in education at Montana State University at Bozeman, accompanied this time also by his young son Warren. Between 1988 and 1997 Mr. Hill served as superintendent of schools for the Lake and Peninsula Borough School District.

Education and achievement have always been important to Mr. Hill; his parents and his grandmother, Mary Ann Trefon, encouraged all of their children to make the most of their school opportunities. After Billy Hill died suddenly in 1946, the idea that education mattered continued to be instilled in the Hill children by their mother and grandmother — with the notion that no one could take away one's education. As a young student Mr. Hill was also inspired to learn by two teachers in particular — Rhoda Thomas, at the Newhalen school, and John Meggitt, at the Levelock school.

When he was very young, Mr. Hill's family moved to the Naknek area where his father was winterman at Libbyville cannery. Billy Hill had not only fished the Naknek River, but had prospected and trapped the length of the Naknek River drainage from the Valley of Ten Thousand Smokes in the Katmai country to the mouth of the river near Libbyville. Morever, many of Mr. Hill's Nondalton relatives fished at Diamond NN cannery in South Naknek. Mr. Hill's father-in-law, Howard Baltzo, worked for the U.S. Fish and Wildlife Service and in the 1950s helped to establish a salmon weir on the Brooks River. In the late 1990s Mr. Hill's son Warren was a backcountry ranger in Katmai National park and Preserve, and he now works in the same capacity for Lake Clark National Park and Preserve. In short, Mr. Hill has roots in the Naknek region that span multiple generations through blood and marriage, combined with his own subsequent adult life as commercial fisherman, hunter-trapper, and educator — all of which make for a knowledgeable individual who has contributed significantly to the betterment of the Bristol Bay region.

Early in his teaching career in Naknek, Mr. Hill was asked to teach a class on local history, but as there was no text to provide guidance he was forced to improvise a course of study. Undeterred, he assigned his students to document their own family histories. What developed were diverse family sagas chronicling a slice of the twentieth century cultural and ethnic mosaic of America and Alaska. Later, while Mr. Hill was Lake and Peninsula superintendent of schools, he was an enthusiastic supporter of a local history text, *Readings from Southwest Alaska*, that was compiled by the National Park Service and published in 1997 by the Alaska Natural History Association for use in the four Bristol Bay area school districts.

Mr. Hill believes the study of local history helps one to understand cultural changes, and this knowledge can offer both solace and guidance for the future. History empowers an individual with a sense of stewardship of local resources and shows how today's people fit into the larger state, national, and international contexts of the modern world. The foregoing text, *A Naknek Chronicle*, in addition, will also assist visitors to the region to gain a taste of the fascinating cultural diversity of the Naknek River and an appreciation for its eventful history.

Mr. Hill is currently working with a grant from the National Science Foundation to encourage school districts to incorporate local traditional knowledge into school curricula, while Dr. Dumond continues to illuminate the prehistory and history of Alaska. Readers can thank both men for the present book. We can hope it will inspire similar studies of other important Alaskan river regions.

John Branson
Park Historian
Lake Clark National Park and Preserve

"Native spear throwing contest, Naknek, Bering Sea, Alaska"
August 1916. Photo courtesy of the San Francisco Maritime National
Historic Park, San Francisco, California, Fort Mason.